10 Secrets All Business Owners Must Know

That Coaches and Marketing Experts Won't Tell You!

by Larry Fisher

COPYRIGHT AND DISCLAIMER

This material is copyright. No part, in whole or in part, may be reproduced by any process, or any other exclusive right exercised, without the permission of Larry Fisher © 2017

LARRY FISHER

Published by:
Leader Publishing Worldwide
19 Axford Bay
Port Moody, BC V3H 3R4
Tel: 1 888 294 9151
Fax: 1 877 575 9151
Website: www.noresults-nofee.com

DISCLAIMER AND/OR LEGAL NOTICES:
While every attempt has been made to verify information provided in this book, neither the author nor the publisher assumes any responsibility for any errors, omissions or inaccuracies.

Any slights of people or organizations are unintentional. If advice concerning legal or related matters is needed, the services of a qualified professional should be sought. This book is not intended as a source of legal or accounting advice. You should be aware of any laws which govern business transactions or other business practices in your state or province.

The income statements and examples are not intended to represent or guarantee that everyone will achieve the same results. Each individual's success will be determined by his or her desire, dedication, effort, and motivation. There are no guarantees you will duplicate the results stated here, you recognize that any business endeavor has inherent risk for loss of capital.

Any reference to any persons or business, whether living or deceased, existing or defunct, is purely coincidental.

PRINTED IN THE USA

DEDICATION

With love to my family Betty, John, Nancy and Bonnie for their support. They shared my excitement for this project, as they do for everything else in my life.

And to the many talented executives and managers with whom I've worked over the years, and from whom I've taken many of the things they've implemented and put into this book. Also, a special thanks to my first business partners Dave Hornbaker, Kent Roberts and Greg McKinstry. In the 80s, I was already a seasoned hotelier, 10 years into managing hotels and so darn confident in my ability to deliver results as a leader, I figured I didn't need strong marketing strategies and tactics. These three taught me otherwise and as a result, helped me discover my passion for leadership development and making marketing a meaningful part of my life.

In a word, they've helped me make this a better book.

To Your Success,

Larry Fisher

CONTENTS

Chapter 1 ... How to Double Your Referrals

Chapter 2 ... Immediate Sales

Chapter 3 ... Profits Through Building a TEAM

Chapter 4 ... Define Your Target Market

Chapter 5 ... Creating a Powerful Offer

Chapter 6 ... Profiting from Internet Marketing

Chapter 7 ... Systemizing Your Business and Developing Effective Processes

Chapter 8 ... How to Create Repeat Business and Have Clients that Pay, Stay and Refer

Chapter 9 ... Risk Reversal to Increase Sales

Chapter 10 ... Profits from Fresh Air

INTRODUCTION

Are you, or your marketing team really thinking strategically about your marketing efforts? If not, look no further for help. By opening this first page you've already taken an important step towards increasing the success of your business. Congratulations in your quest to enhance your business and marketing skills.

Have you ever wondered why some businesses are able to enjoy a healthy mixture of profit and growth while others are limping through on life support? Or why some small businesses are not only able to satisfy their customers, but to successfully create and grow a base of loyal customers, even in a bad economy? Or let's assume you have a limited marketing budget and too many "opportunities" coming at you … how do you determine which, if any, make sense for your business and are worthy of execution?.

For twenty-some years of experience in management and consulting with both large and small businesses of every conceivable ilk, I finally sat down to put pen to paper or keyboard to Word document and when I did, I found myself with an enormous amount of useful marketing material I've used since 1983. This experience is drawn from many different business entities in multiple Industries including VP Operations Director for two Southern California hotel management and development companies; owner of a small real estate investment and brokerage firm, and small business consulting practice. For decades, I used many of the strategies I talk about in this book to develop, reposition, rescue and launch new businesses.

Even though I truly believe we are all 1 or 2 great marketing ideas away from more sales opportunities, in our capitalistic economy there's only one way to make money – you've got to sell something to somebody. The strategies in this book – when implemented with strategy and care – are guaranteed to make you more money with less effort. These are strategies that have helped businesses just like yours make hundreds of thousands of dollars – including your competitors.

I have dedicated my life to business coaching and consulting. Since starting my company to provide direction for small business owners, I have been literally overwhelmed with the demand for marketing, leadership, strategy and for the need of small business operators to surround themselves with someone that cares and who can provide a proper and profitable third-party perspective.

I hope you gain from this book and remember, it does not matter what industry nor type of business you operate (I've been part of Hospitality, Healthcare, Banking, Professional and Real Estate services, and others). That the truths about marketing strategies that I've discovered over the last two-plus decades will help you improve your business. What matters is that you grasp the heart of the principles, the underlying lessons and strategies, that can help grow any operation in any category of business imaginable.

The best time to start is NOW, to steepen your growth curve, to brighten your profit picture and to develop the strategies to lead to success. To this end, I've written this book.

1

How to Double your Referrals

"Stop Selling, Start Helping"
- Zig Ziglar

What if I told you that you could put an inexpensive system in place that would effectively allow your business to grow itself?

For most business owners, a large part of their customer base is comprised of referral customers. These people found out about the company's products or services from the recommendation of a friend or colleague who had a positive experience purchasing from that company.

If your business benefits from referral customers, you will find that these customers arrive ready to buy from you, and tend to buy more often. They also tend to be highly loyal to your product or service.

Seem like great customers to have, don't they?

Referral customers cost less to acquire. Compared to the leads you generate from advertising, direct mail campaigns, and other marketing initiatives, referral customers come to you already qualified and already trusting in the quality of your offering and the respectability of your staff.

With a little effort, and the creation of a formalized system – or strategy – you can not only continue to enjoy referral business, but easily double the number of referral customers that walk through your door. All of this is possible with a minimal investment of time and resources.

Is Your Business a Referral Business?

Referral based businesses benefit from a stream of qualified customers who arrive at their doorstep ready to spend. These businesses put less focus on advertising to generate new leads, and more focus on serving and communicating with their existing customers.

Generally speaking, a referral program can generate outstanding results for nearly any business. Since most referrals do not require any effort, the addition of a strategy and a program will often double or triple the number of qualified referrals that come through a business door.

There are, however, a few types of businesses that will not benefit from a formalized referral strategy. These are businesses with low price points – like fast food restaurants and drugstores. Their customer base is large already, and their efforts would be best spent on increasing the average sale.

A referral program can:

- **Save you time**. Referral strategies – once established – don't require much management or time investment.

- **Deliver more qualified customers.** Your customer arrives with an assumption of trust, and willing to purchase.

- **Improve your reputation.** Your customer's networks likely overlap, and create the potential for a single customer to be referred by two people. This encourages the perception that your business is "the place to go."

- **Speed the sales process.** You will have existing common ground and a reputation with the referred customer.

- **Increase your profit.** You will spend less time and money generating leads, and more time serving customers who have their wallets open.

The Cost of Your Customers

At the risk of stating the obvious, you don't "get" customers, you *buy* them. The money you spend on advertising, direct mail and other promotions ideally results in potential customers walking through your doors.

For example, if you placed an ad for $200, and 20 people make a purchase in response to that ad, you would have paid $10 for each customer.

Referral customers cost you next to nothing. Your existing customer does the work of selling your business to their friend or associate, and you benefit from the sale. Aside from the cost of any referral incentives or coupon production, there is no cost involved at all.

Referral customers cost less and require less time investment than any other customer. That means you can spend that time making them a loyal customer, or a devoted fan.

Groom Your Customers

Referral strategies can allow you to groom your customer base. As we have previously discussed, 80% of your revenue comes from 20% of your customers – these are your ideal customers.

These are also the people you have established as your target market, and are the people you cater your marketing and advertising efforts toward.

You also have a group of customers who make up 80% of your headaches. These are the people who complain the most and spend the least.

Use your referral strategy to get more of your *ideal* customers. Spend more time servicing your ideal customers – do everything you can to make them happy – and less time on your headache customers. You can even ask your headache customers to shop elsewhere.

Then, focus your referral efforts on your ideal customers. Ask them to refer business to you, and reward them for doing so. Try to avoid referrals from your headache customers – chances are you'll just get another headache.

Referral Sources

Take some time to brainstorm all the people who could potentially refer business to you. Think beyond your business, to your extracurricular activities and personal life. There are endless sources of people who are ready and willing to send potential customers your way.

Here are some ideas to get you started:

Past Relationships

No, not romantic relationships. I'm talking about anyone you have previously had a relationship with, but for one reason or another have fallen out of touch. This includes former colleagues, associates, customers, and friends.

Including them in your referral strategy can be as simple as reaching out through the phone or email, and updating them on your latest business initiative or career move. Gently ask at the end of the correspondence to refer anyone who may need your product or service. They will appreciate that you have attempted to re-establish the relationship.

Suppliers and Vendors

Your suppliers and vendors can be a great source for referrals because they presumably deal daily with businesses that are complementary to your own. The opportunities to connect two of their customers in a mutually beneficial relationship are endless. These businesses should be happy to help out - especially if you have been a regular and loyal customer.

Customers

Customers are an obvious source of referrals because they are the people who are dealing with you directly on a regular basis. Often, all you have to do is ask and they will happily provide you with contact information of other interested buyers, or contact those buyers themselves.

Your customers also have a high level of product knowledge when it comes to your business, and are in a great position to really sell the strength of your company. As with any testimonial, the words of your customers are at least 10 times more powerful than any clever headline or marketing piece you could create.

Employees and Associates

Give your employees and associates a reason to have their friends and families shop at your business with a simple incentive program. These people have the most product knowledge and are in the best position to sell you to a potential customer.

This is also a way to tap into an endless network of people. Who do your employees and associates know? Who do their friends and friends of friends know? A referral chain that connects to your employees can be a highly powerful one.

Competitors

This doesn't seem so obvious, but it can work. Your direct competitors are clearly not the ideal source for referrals. However, indirect competitors can refer their clients or potential clients to you if they cannot meet those clients' needs themselves.

For example, if you sell high end lighting fixtures, the low-budget lighting store down the street may be able to refer clients to you, and vice versa. You may wish to offer a finder's fee or incentive to establish this arrangement.

Your Network

Don't be shy about asking your friends and family members for referrals. Too many people do not provide enough information to their inner circle about what they do or what their business does. This doesn't make sense since these are the people who should be the most interested!

Take time to explain clearly what your business is all about, and what your point of difference is. Then just ask them if they know anyone who may benefit from what you are offering. You could even provide your friends and family with an incentive – a gift, a meal, or a portion of the sale.

Associations + Special Interest Groups

This is another place you likely have a network of people who have limited knowledge about what you do or what your business does. The advantage here is that you have a group of people with similar beliefs and values in the same room. Use it!

The Media

Unless a member of the media is a regular customer of yours, or you are in business to serve the media, this may not seem like an obvious choice either.

The opportunity here is to establish a relationship with an editor or journalist and position yourself as an expert in your field or industry. Then, next time they are writing a related story, they can ask to quote you and your opinion. When their audience reads the story, they will perceive your business as the industry leader.

Referral Strategies

A referral strategy is any system you can put in place to generate new leads through existing customers. The ideal way to do this is to create a system that runs itself! Here are some ideas for simple strategies you can begin to implement into your business immediately.

Just Ask

This may seem simple and obvious, but it's true. Be open with your customers and associates, and simply ask them if they can refer any of their friends or associates to you. Make it part of doing business with you, and your customers will grow to expect the question. Or, let them know in advance that you'll be asking at a later date.

Remember that this can include potential customers – even if they don't buy from you. The reason they chose not to purchase may have nothing to do with your business; any person who has begun to or actually done business with you can refer to you another person.

Offer Incentives

When you speak to your customers, when you ask them for something, you typically try to answer the question "what's in it for me?" before they ask it.

The same is true when you ask your customers for a referral. Incentive-based referral strategies work wonders, and can easily be implemented as part of a customer loyalty program, or as part of your existing customer relations systems.

Consider offering customers who successfully refer clients to you discounts on products, free products or services, or gifts. Offer incentives relative to the number of referrals, or the success rate of each referral.

This can have a spin-off effect, as your referral customers may become motivated to continue the referral chain. They too will be interested in the incentives you have provided and will tell their friends about your business.

Be Proactive

The only way your referral program will work is if you put some effort into it, and maintain some level of ongoing effort.

Here are some ideas:

- Put a referral card or coupon in every shopping bag that leaves your store

- Promote gift certificates during peak seasons
- Offer free information seminars to existing customers, and ask them to bring a friend
- Host a closed-door sale for your top 20 customers and their friends

Provide Great Customer Service

An easy way to encourage referral business is to treat every potential customer with exemplary customer service. Since the art of customer service is lost is many communities, people are often impressed by simple added touches and conveniences. That alone will encourage them to refer your business to their network.

Stay in Touch

Make sure you are staying in touch with all of your potential and converted customers. Through newsletters, direct mail, or the Internet, keep your business name at the top of the minds, ahead of the competition.

Even if they have already purchased from you, and may not need to purchase for some time, a newsletter or email can be a simple reminder that your business is out there. If someone in their network is looking for the product or service, it will be more likely that your customer will refer your business to the competition.

2

Immediate Sales

"If you are going to be remembered for having gotten things done, you're a sales person. You're a sales person in the morning, at lunch, at dinner and you dream about it at night. Sales ... sales ... sales."
- Tom Peters

If you're a business owner, you're also a salesperson.

You've had to sell the bank to get them to loan you your start-up capital. You've had to sell the best employees on why they should work for your business. You've had to convince your business partner, spouse, and friends why your business idea is a good one.

Now you have to repeatedly sell your product or service to your customers.

The ability to sell effectively and efficiently is one that every successful business owner has cultivated and continues to develop. It can be a complicated and time-consuming task; one that you will have to continually work on throughout your career in order to be – and stay – successful.

Fortunately, making sales is a step-by-step process that can be learned, customized, and continuously improved. There is a wide range of tools available to help and support your sales efforts.

You don't have to be the most outgoing, enthusiastic person to be successful at sales. You don't even have to be a good public speaker. All you need is an understanding of the basic sales process and a genuine passion for what you are selling.

Sales 101

As I said before, making sales is a process. There are clear, step-by-step actions that can be taken and result in a sale.

The sales process varies according to the type of business, type of customers and type of product or service that is offered; however, the core steps are the same. Similarly, sales training varies from individual to individual, but the core skills and abilities remain the same.

Here is a basic seven-step process that you can follow, or fine tune to suit your unique products and services. Remember that each step is important, and builds on the previous step. Becoming adept at each step is essential, instead of solely focusing on closing the sale.

1. Preparation

Make sure you have prepared for your meeting, presentation, or a day on the sales floor. You have complete control of this part of the sales process, so it is important to do everything you can to set the stage for your success.

- Understand your product or service inside and out.
- Prepare all the necessary materials, and organize them neatly.
- Keep your place of business tidy and organized. Reface product on shelves.
- Ensure you appear professional and well-groomed.
- Do some research on your potential client and brainstorm to find common ground.

2. Build a Relationship

The first few minutes you spend with a potential customer sets the stage for the rest of your interaction. First impressions are everything. Your goal in the second step is to relax the customer and begin to develop a relationship with them. Establishing a real relationship with your customer will create trust.

- Make a great first impression: shake hands, make eye contact, and introduce yourself.
- Remain confident and professional, but also personable.
- Mirror their speech and behavior.
- Begin with general questions and small talk.

- Show interest in them and their place of business.
- Notice and comment on positives.
- Find some common ground with which to relate.

3. Discuss Needs + Wants

Once you have spent a few moments getting to know your prospect, start asking open-ended questions to discover some of their needs and wants. If they have come to you on the sales floor, ask what brought them into the store. If you are meeting them to present your product or service, ask why they are interested in, or what criteria they have in mind for that product or service.

- If you are making a sales presentation, ask for a few moments at the outset to outline the purpose of your visit, as well as how you have structured the presentation.
- Listen intently, and repeat back information you are not sure you understand.
- Ask open-ended questions to get them talking. The longer they talk, the more insight they are providing you with their needs and purchase motivations.
- Ask clarifying questions about their responses.
- If you become sure the customer is going to buy your product or service, begin to ask questions specific to the offering. i.e., what size/color do you prefer?

4. Present the Solution

Once you have a solid understanding of what they are looking for, or what issue they are looking to resolve, you can begin to present the solution: your product or service.

- Explain how your product or service will solve their problem or meet their needs. If several products apply, begin by presenting the mid-level product.
- Illustrate your points with anecdotes about other happy customers, or awards the product or service has earned.
- Use hypothetical examples featuring your customer. Encourage them to picture a scenario after their purchase.
- Begin by describing the benefits of the product, then follow-up with features and advantages.
- Watch your customer's behavior as you speak, and ask further qualifying questions in response to body language and verbal comments.
- Give the customer an opportunity to ask you questions or provide feedback about each product or service after you have described or explained it.
- Ask closed-ended questions to gain agreement.

5. Overcome Objections

As you present the product or service, take note of potential objections by asking open-ended questions and monitoring body language. Expect that objections will arise and prepare for it. Consider brainstorming a list of all potential objections, and writing down your responses.

- Repeat the objection back to the customer to ensure you understand them correctly.
- Empathize with what they have said, and then provide a response that overcomes the objection.
- Confirm that the answer you have provided has overcome their objection by repeating yourself.

The Eight Most Common Objections
The product or service does not seem valuable to me. There is no reason for me to act now. I will wait. It's safest not to make a decision right away. There is not enough money for the purchase. The competitor or another department offers a better product. There are internal issues between people or departments. The relationship with the decision maker is strained. There is an existing contract in place with another business.

6. Close

This is an important part of the sales process that should be handled delicately. Deciding when to close is a judgment call that must be made in the moment during the sale. Ideally, you have presented a solution to their problem, overcome objections, and you now have the customer in a place where they are ready to buy.

Here are some questions to ask before you close the sale:

- Does my prospect agree that there is value in my product or service?
- Does my prospect understand the features and benefits of the product or service?

- Are there any remaining objections that must be handled?
- Are there other factors that could influence my prospect's decision to buy?
- Have I minimized the risk involved in the purchase, and provided some level of urgency?

Once you have determined it is time to make the sale, here are some sample statements you can use to get the process rolling:

- So, should we get started?
- Shall I grab a new one from the back?
- If you just give me your credit card, I can take care of the transaction while you continue browsing.
- When would you like the product delivered?
- We can begin next month if we receive payment by the end of the week.
- Can I email you a draft of the contract tomorrow?

7. Service + Follow-up

Once you have made the sale, your work is not over. You want to ensure that that customer will become a loyal, repeat customer and that they will refer their friends to your business.

Ask them to be in your customer database, and keep in touch with regular newsletters. Follow up with a phone call or drop by to ask how they are enjoying the product or service, and if they have any further questions or needs you can assist them with.

This contact opportunity will also allow you to ask for a referral or an upsell. At the very least, it will ensure you are continuing to foster and build a relationship with the client.

Up selling

Upselling is simply inviting your customers to spend more money in your business by purchasing additional products or services. This could include more of the same product, complementary products, or impulse items.

Regardless, upselling is an effective way to increase profits and create loyal clients – without spending any money to acquire the business. These clients are already purchasing from you – which means they perceive value in what you have to offer – so take the information you have gained in the sales process and offer them a bit more.

You experience up selling on a daily basis. From "do you want fries with that?" to "have you heard about our product protect program?" companies across the globe have tapped into and trained their staff on the value of the upsell.

Up-selling is truly rooted in good customer service. If your client purchases a new computer printer, you'll need to make sure they have the cords required to connect it to the computer, regular and photo paper, and color and black and white ink.

If you don't suggest these items, they may arrive home and realize they do not have all the materials needed to use the product. They may choose to purchase those materials somewhere closer, cheaper, or more helpful.

Customer education is another form of up-selling. What if your customer doesn't realize that you sell a variety of printer paper and stationery in addition to computer hardware like printers? Take every opportunity to educate your customer on the products and services you offer that may be of interest to them.

An effective way of implementing an upsell system into your business is simply by creating add-on checklists for the products or services you offer. Each item has a list of related items that your customer may need. This will encourage your staff to develop the habit of asking for the upsell.

Other up-sell strategies can be implemented:

- **At the point of sale**. This is a great place for impulse items like candy, flashlights, nail scissors, etc.

- **In a newsletter**. This is an effective strategy for customer education.

- **In your merchandising**. Place strips of impulse items near related items. For example, paper clips with paper and pens near binders.

- **Over the phone**. If someone is placing an order for delivery, offer additional items in the same shipment for convenience.

- **With new products**. Feature each new product or service that you offer prominently in your business, and ask your staff to mention it to every customer.

Sales Team

Employing a team of strong salespeople

What Makes a Good Salesperson?

There are a lot of salespeople out there – but what qualities and skills make a great salesperson? These are the attributes you will want to find or develop in your team:

- Willingness to continuously learn and improve sales skills
- Sincerity in relating to customers and providing solutions to their objectives
- An understanding of the company's big picture
- A communication style that is direct, polite, and professional
- Honesty and respect for other team members, customers, as well as the competition.
- Ability to manage time
- Enthusiastic
- Inquisitive
- A great listener
- Ability to quickly interpret, analyze, and respond to information during the sales process

- Ability to connect and develop relationships of trust with potential clients
- Professional appearance

Team Building – Keeping Your Team Together

In many businesses, Sales is a department or a whole team of people who work together to generate leads and convert customers. Effective management of your sales team is a skill every business owner should cultivate.

Team building, recruitment and training will be discussed in later sections, but take some time to consider the following aspects of managing a sales team:

Communication
- Are targets and results regularly reviewed?
- Are opportunities for input regularly provided?
- Do sales staff members have a clear understanding of what is expected?
- Do all staff members know daily, weekly, and quarterly targets?

Performance Management
- Are sales staff members motivated to reach targets?
- Are sales staff recognized and rewarded once those targets are reached?
- Are there opportunities for skills training and development?

- Do staff members have a broad and comprehensive product or industry knowledge?
- Is there an opportunity for growth within the company?
- Is performance regularly reviewed?

Operations
- Do you have a solid understanding of your sales numbers (revenue, profit, margins)?
- Are your sales processes regularly reviewed?
- Do you have a variety of sales scripts prepared?
- Do you measure conversion rates?
- How are your leads generated?

Sales Tools

Every salesperson should have an arsenal of tools on hand to assist them in the sales process. These tools can act as aids while a sale is taking place, or help to foster continual learning and development of the salesperson's skills and approach.

The list below includes some popular sales tools. Add to this list with other resources that are specific to your business or industry.

Tool	Description + Benefit
Scripts	Used for incoming and outgoing telemarketing, cold calls, door-to-door sales, in-store sales Create several different scripts throughout your business Maintains consistency in your sales approach Revise and renew your scripts regularly
Presentation Materials	High-quality information about your product or service Forms: PowerPoint presentation, brochure, product sheets, proposal Serves as an outline of your sales presentation, and keeps you on task
Colleagues	A source of help and advice, especially when you are on the same team or sell similar products Also a source of support
Customer Databases	An accurate, up-to-date database of customer contact information and contact history Used to stay in touch with clients Can also be used for direct mail and follow-up telemarketing
The Internet	A powerful resource for sales help and advice Information to help improve your sales process Online sales coaching Source for product knowledge
Ongoing Training	Constant improvement of your sales skills Constant increase in product knowledge Investment in yourself and your company

8 Tips for Better Sales

- **Dress for the sale.** Dress professionally, appear well put together and maintain good hygiene. Ensure you are not only dressed professionally, but *appropriately*. Would your client feel more comfortable if you wore a suit, or jeans and blazer?

- **Speak their language.** Show you understand their industry or culture, and use phrases your customer understands. This may require researching industry jargon or common phrases. Remember to avoid using words and phrases that are used in the sales process: sold, contract, telemarketing, finance, interest, etc. Doing so will help break down the salesperson/customer barrier.

- **Ooze positivity**. Show up or answer the phone with a smile, and leave your personal or business issues behind. Be enthusiastic about what you have to offer, and how that offering will benefit your customer. Reflect this not only in your voice but also in your body language.

- **Deliver a strong pitch or presentation**. Be confident and convincing. Leave self-doubt at the door, and walk in assuming the sale. Take time to explain complex concepts, and always connect what you're saying to your audience in a specific way.

- **Be a poster child for good manners**. Accept any amenity you're offered, listen intently, don't interrupt, don't show up late, have a strong handshake, and give everyone you are speaking to equal attention.

- **Avoid sensitive subjects.** Politics, religion, swearing, sexual innuendos and racial comments are absolutely off-limits. So are negative comments about other customers or the competition.

- **Create a real relationship.** Icebreakers and small talk are not just to pass the time before your presentation. They are how relationships get established. Show genuine interest in everything your customer has to say. Ask questions about topics you know they are passionate. Speak person to person, not salesperson to customer. Remember everything.

- **Know more than you need to.** Impress clients with comprehensive knowledge – not only of your product or service – but also of the people who use that product or service, and industry trends. Be seen as an expert in order to build trust and respect.

3

Profits Through Building a TEAM
(Together Everyone Achieves More)

"Coming together is a beginning. Keeping together is progress. Working together is success."
-Henry Ford

The people you employ contribute – directly or indirectly – on a daily basis to the strength and vitality of your business. You can't run your business alone, so you rely on their skills and support.

In simpler words, your employees help you to make money.

But your employees are not just the people who arrive at your office every day and exchange effort for a paycheck. Their role is not just to build capacity and sell more or serve more.

Your employees are part of a potentially powerful group of people that you can leverage to put your business on the fast track to success. Your staff is more than the people who work for you. They are actually members of your team – the group of people who are collectively working to achieve the same objective, or reach the same vision.

I say they are more than just employees because their collective, cohesive value is much higher than their individual worth.

We all know that more people working on the same task will ensure the task is completed faster. In business, when you have more people working together on the same task, you save time, increase brainpower, and ultimately, **make more money**.

Corporate Culture

Corporate Culture has become a common buzzword when it comes to building a successful business, and rightly so.

Your corporate culture is the environment in which you run your business and the environment in which your team members work. It is rooted in the vision, mission and beliefs of the organization, and dictates the "kind of office" and "kind of people" that work in that office.

Corporate culture is something that typically develops organically. The business owner and senior employees create a positive or negative environment based solely on who they are as people and how they behave as leaders. You simply can't avoid creating some type of corporate culture when you run a business.

You can, however, avoid creating a negative or unproductive corporate culture. Whether you are just starting out or seeking to improve your workplace, you do have control over the type of environment in which you run your business.

Like most things in business, this won't happen overnight. However, with a clear idea of where you want to go, and what you want to create, you'll be well on your way to getting there.

Vision

Your company's vision statement should be a bold, clear, short sentence that every single one of your employees knows and understands. It is a roadmap to your idea of success; if you don't know what that looks like, how will you know when you achieve it?

If your goal is to create a highly profitable company – what does highly profitable mean? $1 million in annual sales? $3 million in annual profit?

Do you seek to become the industry leader in sprocket production? How will this be measured? How many sprockets will you have to produce to reach this goal?

The vision statement is a short summary of the long-term objective of the company. What the company will look like, produce, achieve; it is how you know the company is "successful."

Many companies either do not have a vision statement or they keep it a secret from their employees. It is only discussed in board meetings or management meetings. For a team to collectively work toward a destination (your vision), it needs to be compelling, and it should be communicated effectively so that everyone WANTS to get on the "company bus" to get there. They need to know what the big picture objective is – where you're taking the bus. They need to have buy-in for the company's direction and be effectively communicated with on a regular basis.

Be proud of your vision. Keep it visible for staff – post it on the wall, include it in internal communications, and connect day-to-day activities to it as often as possible.

Sample Vision Statements

Here are some real examples of corporate vision statements:

"At Microsoft, our mission and values are to help people and businesses through the world realize their potential." – Microsoft

"Give every customer a reason to believe…STAPLES Business Depot—That was easy!" – Staples Canada

"To build the largest and most complete Amateur Radio community site on the Internet." – eHam.net

Creating a Vision Statement

The process of creating a vision statement is something that you can work through alone, or in collaboration with your team. It is highly recommended to review the draft vision statement with your employees to ensure they understand and support the goals and objectives of the company.

Keep the following points in mind when crafting your vision statement:

- **Think big** – Why did you start or buy this business? What was your dream or purpose in doing so?
- **Think long-term** – Vision statements should last five to 10 or even 25 years
- **Be specific** – Use numbers, dates, rating systems and other ways of measuring success
- **Be succinct** – Use clear, short, simple sentences that are easy to repeat and remember

An effective and "Compelling Vision" should be:
- **Perceptive** - based on insight analysis of the present situation facing the company
- **A good choice** – selected from well-considered options
- **Appealing** - to the deep desires of those who work within the company
- **A clear statement** - of the **MOTIVATING** force that drives the organization forward
- **Achievable**

Mission

Your mission statement is a general description of how you are going to achieve your vision. This is a longer and more detailed statement that should include what your business does, for whom, and why (how you are different from, or better than, your competition).

Sample Mission Statements

"The Mission of McGill University is the advancement of learning through teaching, scholarship and service to society: by offering to outstanding undergraduate and graduate students the best education available; by carrying out scholarly activities judged to be excellent when measured against the highest international standards; and by providing service to society in those ways for which we are well-suited by virtue of our academic strengths." – McGill University, Montreal, Canada

"Starbucks purchases and roasts high-quality whole bean coffees and sells them along with fresh, rich-brewed, Italian style espresso beverages, a variety of pastries and confections, and coffee-related accessories and equipment -- primarily through its company-operated retail stores. In addition to sales through our company-operated retail stores, Starbucks sells whole bean coffees through a specialty sales group and supermarkets. Additionally, Starbucks produces and sells bottled Frappuccino® coffee drink and a line of premium ice creams through its joint venture partnerships and offers a line of innovative premium teas produced by its wholly owned subsidiary, Tazo Tea Company. The Company's objective is to establish Starbucks as the most recognized and respected brand in the world." – Starbucks

Creating Your Mission Statement:

Here is a recommended process for completing your mission statement:

Step One: List your company's internal strengths and weaknesses; what do you do well? What do you need to work on, or avoid doing?

Step Two: Who are your primary customers? Describe the types of customers you serve – both internal and external.

Step Three: What do your customers think of your strengths? What strengths are most important to them? Go ahead and ask them if you need to.

Step Four: Connect the strength that each customer values with its customer type. Write it in a sentence. Combine any redundancies.

Step Five: Organize your sentences in order of importance

Step Six: Combine your sentences into a paragraph or two. Elaborate on points as needed. This is your draft mission statement.

Step Six: Consult with your staff and customers, and ask for their feedback. Do employees support the statement? Can they act on it? Do customers want to do business with a company with this mission statement? Does it make sense?

Step Seven: Incorporate the feedback received, and refine the statement until you are happy with it. Then publish it – everywhere.

Culture or Values Statements

Your culture or values statement is the next step in the process. It describes how you and your staff will go about taking action (your mission statement) to achieve your objective (your vision statement).

Much like every family has their own belief system and way of doing things – from cooking to cleaning to raising kids – every company has their own set of values when it comes to running a business. It reflects the unique personality of the organization.

Sample Culture Statement

Our Culture
* *Values-based leadership. Our Credo outlines the values that provide the foundation of how we act as a corporation and as individual employees so that we continue to put the needs of the people we serve first.*

* *Diversity. It's our individual differences that make us stronger as a whole. We recognize the strength and value that comes when collaborative relationships are built between people of different ages, race, gender, religion, nationality, sexual orientation, physical ability, thinking style, personal backgrounds and all other attributes that make each person unique.*

* *Innovation. True innovation can only be fostered within a supportive environment that values calculated risk in order to achieve the maximum reward. At Johnson & Johnson Inc., we encourage and reward innovative thinking, innovative solutions and an innovative approach in all that we do.*

Passion. The deep desire to enrich people's lives – by delivering quality products and remarkable experiences that make their lives easier, healthier and more joyful.

Collaboration. The unwavering belief that great results depend on the ability to create trusting relationships.

Courage. The fearless pursuit of the unproven, unknown possibility – the willingness to take great risks for the benefit of the greater good.
- Johnson & Johnson Canada

Creating Your Culture Statement

Involve your team in creating your company's culture or values statement. Generally, this is a point-form document that reflects the beliefs of the company, its employees, and its customers.

It can be helpful to think about the type of people you currently employ, as well as the ones you may wish to employ. What are they like? What are their belief systems? What are their most important values?

Remember that the culture or values statement is usually the longest of the three statements – and that's okay.

Your Team Leaders

The strength of a team lies in the strength of the people who lead it. No group of people is effective without strong leadership, just like no business is effective without a strong owner or management team.

Building a strong team means knowing who your leaders are – both in the job description and their natural ability.

Understanding the strength of your natural leaders and the skills of your natural followers will allow you to strategically structure your team for maximum effectiveness and efficiency. It will give you insight into who is best suited for management promotions and project management; which team members have the ability to assemble and motivate their peers.

Your leaders need to have a high degree of passion for your product or service, and truly believe in the company's vision. They need to be able to handle a high level of responsibility and manage a range of people to achieve a common goal.

Your leaders are your team builders. They present new ideas, build consensus, and encourage the involvement of others.

Types of Leaders

Simply speaking, there are four main types, or styles, of leaders. Chances are, you've experienced each type at some point in your career.

Type	Description	Ideal Use
Autocratic	Classical or "old-school" approach Manager holds all power and decision-making authority No employee consultation or input Orders are obeyed Rewards/punishment structure	New, untrained employees Detailed orders and instructions are required No other leadership style has been effective Limited time available Department restructuring High production requirements
Bureaucratic	"By the book" approach All is done to specific procedures/policies All tasks outside policies referred to higher management	Routine tasks performed Standards and procedures need to be communicated regularly Safety or training Cash handling Dangerous equipment
Laissez-faire	"Hands-off" approach Employees have almost total freedom Little direction or guidance is provided Employees must make own decisions, set own goals Employees must solve own problems	Highly skilled and experienced employees Employees are highly driven and ambitious Consultants are being managed Employees are trustworthy
Democratic	"Participatory approach" Employees part of decision-making process Employees well-informed Leader has final say, but involved others Collaborative approach Encourages employee development with guidance and assistance from leader Leader recognizes and rewards achievement	Collaborative environment Employee development and growth is the focus Changes or problems affect employees and require their input to create a solution Team building and participation is encouraged

Communication

The only way to build and maintain a strong team is through strong, consistent communication. This is often an overlooked or neglected aspect of business management, and is easily forgotten during periods of high stress or heavy workload.

Avoid letting communication fall on the back burner by creating a regular meeting schedule – and sticking to it. Depending on the size and type of your business, daily, weekly, or monthly team meetings are an important cornerstone of a strong team.

Regularly scheduled team meetings are like Sunday dinners with a busy family. They give you – the owner – a regular forum with your staff to implement company-wide training initiatives, announce results, establish goals and targets, or share new visions or directions. They also give your staff a forum to share feedback and air grievances.

Effective Team Meetings

By now you're probably thinking, "Sure, I hear some company's team meetings are effective, but we tried them and it didn't work," or "I held regular team meetings, but after a while, no one showed up."

There is a difference between team meetings held for the sake of having team meetings and well-prepared team meetings with a purpose.

You need to start holding team meetings with a purpose.

Establish a Schedule That Everyone Can Commit To

Scheduling is potentially the biggest challenge when trying to set up a team meeting. Often, all of your staff members are busy going in eight different directions to fulfill their roles and operating on dramatically different schedules.

This is one reason why regular team meetings are important. Ad hoc meetings require ad hoc scheduling and reduce the likelihood that all your team members will be able to attend.

Ask your team to block off one hour (or two) each week (or month) for the team meeting in a time slot that is convenient for everyone. Establish a clear attendance expectation from everyone. This will exclude that time slot from the scheduling of other meetings and avoid conflict.

If you find that a team meeting is not necessary one week, you can always cancel it.

Know Your Purpose

Each team meeting should have a purpose and clear objectives. Is it to educate? Build consensus? Gather feedback?

Once you have established a purpose for a particular meeting, send an agenda to your staff confirming the meeting and outlining your objectives. This is a good time to ask if anyone has a subject they would like to raise at the meeting.

If you find you do not have a clear purpose or objective, ask yourself if a team meeting is the best use of time for that week and consider postponing it to the next regularly scheduled time slot.

Plan Each and Every Minute

The biggest complaint from employees about team meetings is the length. Too often team meetings run out of control and end up taking three hours instead of one. You will quickly lose team focus and respect for the regular meeting this way. By establishing a clear agenda and staying on topic, you can run an efficient, succinct meeting.

Your detailed agenda should include:

- meeting purpose or objective
- list of topics and associated speakers
- list of decisions that need to be made/agreed to
- time allocation for each topic
- opportunity for additional topics at the end

Circulate your draft agenda in advance of the meeting, and request input and feedback. When all team members have reviewed, and contributed to the agenda, you will increase their level of ownership and buy-in into the process.

Establish the Facilitator

Choose one person to chair the meeting and keep it on track. This is generally the business owner or a senior member of the team with some authority over junior staff and a high level of respect.

It is the responsibility of the facilitator – or chairperson – to create an environment of open dialogue and trust and to keep the meeting on schedule.

Create a Follow-up Schedule

Assign the task of taking detailed meeting minutes to a team member – or rotate this responsibility on a regular basis. It is important to record what happens in team meetings, just as you would in a client-related business meeting.

In the minutes, establish a system for tracking the action items that arise from decisions made in the meeting. This can be set up as a simple chart:

Decision	Action	Responsibility	Deadline

Make sure that these responsibilities are assigned and agreed upon in the meeting, and clear deadlines are established. Reviewing or following up on this chart can serve as a regular topic during team meetings.

Circulate meeting minutes to all attendees and ask for input or revisions. You may wish to circulate meeting minutes with the agenda for the next team meeting and gather feedback at the same time.

Motivations + Incentives

A big challenge in team building is coming up with new ways to foster and maintain a high level of motivation. How do you keep teams of people excited and driven to succeed over long periods of time? How do you keep your team motivated to improve their performance, and increase their achievements?

It is important to note that we're not just talking about individuals, but teams of people working together. It is fairly simple to motivate a single person, but an entire team of motivated people will generate significantly higher results.

The key here is to give incentives for individual and team accomplishments. Incentives that reward based on collective achievement require people to work together and motivate each other to succeed.

Before we start talking about monetary and incentive-based rewards, it's important to look at motivational factors that are not incentive-driven.

Room to Work

Employees who feel their managers and supervisors believe and trust in their abilities are happier and will always perform at a higher level than those who do not. They are motivated to "prove them right" and feel supported in their efforts.

Micromanagement quickly reduces morale. It is essential that you and your managers clearly express confidence in your team members. You hired them to do a job, perform a role, so you must ensure they have the space to do so.

When you put effective systems in place and establish clear expectations, you create a clear context or boundary system for employees to work within. They understand the decision-making hierarchy, and the general way 'things are done around here.'

Your team should be encouraged to take initiative and to take risks within this context. You have hired your team based on their skills and intellectual capabilities, and thus should be able to trust in their choices and decision-making abilities.

Incentives

Incentives are great motivators. An incentive is a reason to perform or act in a certain way. For example, if your team increases sales by 40% by month's end, they will be treated to an expensive dinner.

Incentives need to be specific and have deadlines in order to be effective. In the example above, sales need to increase by 40% by the end of the month in order for the team to receive their dinner. If sales only increase by 30%, or if they increase by 40% at the end of the second month, the team does not earn their reward.

Time-specific incentives increase the sense of urgency and encourage staff to work harder to achieve the objective. If the incentive is not time-bound, there is no reason to work faster or harder, since staff will assume they will reach their milestone "eventually."

Rarity is also a key component of effective incentive-based team building. If the reward is ongoing (i.e., if staff receive an expensive dinner every month sales are over $75,000), then "there's always next time." There is a lesser incentive to push performance to receive the reward. Some team members may care one month, but not the next.

Monetary Incentives

Bonuses and salary increases are a popular way to give your team an incentive to perform. These can include:

- Commissions
- Bonuses for completing a challenging project, or hitting a target
- Rewards for highest producing employee
- Salary increases based on met targets

It's up to you how you choose to structure your monetary incentives, based on your budget and resources. Remember to ensure that the terms of each incentive are clearly outlined and that both parties (you and your employee) understand the agreement.

Gift Rewards

Physical, tangible gifts are an inexpensive way to reward your team for achievements and improvement. These rewards show that you have given some level of thought to what they might enjoy or appreciate in exchange for a job well done. They're also a great way to surprise employees.

Here are some ideas:

- Spa gift certificates
- Books – *consider motivational or business-related topics*
- CDs or DVDs
- Meals – lunch or breakfast
- Other gift certificates – gas, food, meals, local shops
- Movie or theater tickets
- Weekend getaway – hotel, meals, etc.
- Flowers
- Gym memberships

4

Define Your Target Market

"The aim of marketing is to know and understand the customer so well the product or service fits him and sells itself."
- Peter Drucker

What is a Target Market?

Many businesses can't answer the question: *Who is your target market?* They have often made the fatal assumption that *everyone* will want to purchase their product or service with the right marketing strategy.

A target market is simply the group of customers or clients who will purchase a specific product or service. This group of people all have something in common, often age, gender, hobbies, or location.

Your target market then, is the people who will buy your offering. This includes both existing and potential customers, all of whom are motivated to do one of three things:

- Fulfill a need
- Solve a problem
- Satisfy a desire

To build, maintain, and grow your business, you need to know who your customers are, what they do, what they like, and why they would buy your product or service. Getting this wrong – or not taking the time to get it right – will cost you time, money, and potentially the success of your business.

The Importance of Knowing Your Target Market

Knowledge and understanding of your target market are the keystones in the arch of your business. Without it, your product or service positioning, pricing, marketing strategy, and eventually, your business could very quickly fall apart.

If you don't intimately know your target market, you run the risk of making mistakes when it comes to establishing pricing, product mix, or service packages. Your marketing strategy will lack direction, and produce mediocre results at best. Even if your marketing message and unique selling proposition (USP) are clear, and your brochure is perfectly designed, it means nothing unless it arrives in the hands (or ears) of the right people.

Determining your target market takes time and careful diligence. While it often starts with a best guess, assumptions cannot be relied on and research is required to confirm original ideas. Your target market is not always your ideal market.

Once you build an understanding of who your target market is, keep up with your market research. Having your finger on the pulse of their motivations and drivers – which naturally change – will help you to anticipate needs or wants and evolve your business.

Types of Markets

Consumer

The Consumer Market includes those general consumers who buy products and services for personal use, or for use by family and friends. This is the market category you or I fall into when we're shopping for groceries or clothes, seeing a movie in the theater, or going out for lunch. Retailers focus on this market category when marketing their goods or services.

Institutional

The Institutional Market serves society and provides products or services for the benefit of society. This includes hospitals, non-profit organizations, government organizations, schools and universities. Members of the Institutional Market purchase products to use in the provision of services to people in their care.

Business to Business (B2B)

The B2B Market is just what it seems to be: businesses that purchase the products and services of other business to run their operations. These purchases can include products that are used to manufacture other products (raw or technical), products that are needed for daily operations (such as office supplies), or services (such as accounting, shredding, and legal).

Reseller

This market can also be called the "Intermediary Market" because it consists of businesses that act as channels for goods and services between other markets. Goods are purchased and sold for a profit – without any alterations. Members of this market include wholesalers, retailers, resellers, and distributors.

Determining Your Target Market

Product / Service Investigation

The process for determining your target market starts by examining exactly what your offering is, and what the average customer's motivation for purchasing it is. Start by answering the following questions:

Does your offering meet a basic need?	
Does your offering serve a particular want?	
Does your offering fulfill a desire?	
What is the lifecycle of your product service?	

What is the availability of your offering?	
What is the cost of the average customer's purchase?	
What is the lifecycle of your offering?	
How many times or how often will customers purchase your offering?	
Do you foresee any upcoming changes in your industry or region that may affect the sale of your offering (positive/negative)?	

Market Investigation

- **On the ground.** Spend some time on the ground researching who your target market might be. If you're thinking about opening a coffee shop, hang out in the neighborhood at different times of the day to get a sense of the people who live, work, and play in the neighborhood. Notice their age, gender, clothing, and any other indications of income and activities.

- **At the competition.** Who is your direct competitor targeting? Is there a small niche that is being missed? Observing the clientele of your competition can help to build an understanding of your target market, regardless of whether it is the same or opposite. For example, if you own a children's clothing boutique and the majority of middle-class mothers shop at the local department store, you may wish to focus on higher-income families as your target market.

- **Online.** Many cities and towns – or at least regions – have demographic information available online. Research the ages, incomes, occupations, and other key pieces of information about the people who live in the area you operate your business. From this data, you will gain an understanding of the size of your total potential market.

- **With existing customers.** Talk to your existing customers through focus groups or surveys. This is a great way to gather demographic and behavioral information, as well as genuine feedback about product or service quality and other information that will be useful in a business or marketing strategy.

Who is Your Market?

Based on your product/service and market investigations, you will be able to piece together a basic picture of your target market, and some of their general characteristics. Record some notes here. At this point, you may wish to be as specific as possible, or maintain some generalities. You can further segment your market in the next section.

Consumer Target Market Framework

Market Type:	Consumer
Gender:	☐ Male ☐ Female
Age Range:	
Purchase Motivation:	☐ Meet a Need ☐ Serve a Want ☐ Fulfill a Desire
Activities:	
Income Range:	
Marital Status:	
Location:	☐ Neighborhood ☐ City ☐ Region ☐ Country
Other Notes:	

Institutional Target Market Framework

Market Type:	Institutional
Institution Type:	☐ Hospital ☐ Non-profit ☐ School ☐ University ☐ Charity ☐ Government ☐ Church
Purchase Motivation:	☐ Operational Need ☐ Client Want ☐ Client Desire
Purpose of Institution:	
Institution's Client Base:	
Size:	
Location:	☐ Neighborhood ☐ City ☐ Region ☐ Country
Other Notes:	

B2B Target Market Framework

Market Type:	Business to Business (B2B)
Company Size:	
Number of Employees:	
Purchase Motivation:	☐ Operations Need ☐ Strategy ☐ Functionality
Annual Revenue:	
Industry:	
Location(s):	
Purpose of Business:	
People, Culture & Values:	
Other Notes:	

Reseller Target Market Framework

Market Type:	Reseller
Industry:	
Client Base:	
Purchase Motivation:	☐ Operations Need ☐ Client Wants ☐ Functionality
Annual Revenue:	

Age:	
Location:	☐ Neighborhood ☐ City ☐ Region ☐ Country
Other Notes:	

Your Target Market: Putting It Together

Based on the information you gather from your product/service and market investigations, you should have a clear vision of your realistic target market. Here are a few examples of how this information is put together and conclusions are drawn:

Target Market Sample 1: Consumer Market

Business: Baby Clothing Boutique	**Business Purpose:** *Meet a need* (provide clothing for infants and children aged 0 to 5 years) *Serve a want* (clothing is brand name only, and has a higher price point than the competition)
Market Type: Consumer	
Gender: Women	
Marital Status: Married	
Market Observations: Located on Main Street of Anytown, a street that is seeing many new boutiques open up, proximate to the main shopping mall two blocks from popular mid-range restaurant that is busy at lunch	**Industry Predictions:** Large number of new housing developments in the city and surrounding areas. Two new schools in construction expect to see an influx of new families move to town from Anycity
Competition Observations: Baby clothing also available at two local department stores, and one second-hand shop on opposite side of town	**Online Research:** Half of Anytown's population is female, and 25% have children under the age of 15 years Anytown's population is expected to increase by 32% within three years The average household income for Anytown is $75,000 annually

TARGET MARKET:

The target market can then be described as married mothers with children under five years old, between the ages of 25 and 45, who have recently moved to Anytown from Anycity, and have a household income of at least $100K annually.

Target Market Sample 2: B2B Market

Business: Confidential Paper Shredding	**Target Business Size:** Small to medium
Market Type: B2B (Business to Business)	**Target Business Revenue:** $500K to $1M
Business Purpose: *Meet an operations need* (provide confidential on-site shredding services for business documents)	**Target Business Type:** Produce or handle a variety of sensitive paper documentation Accountants, lawyers, real estate agents, etc.
Market Observations: There are two main areas of office buildings and industrial warehouses in Anycity Three more office towers are being constructed and will be completed this year	**Industry Predictions:** The professional sector is seeing revenue growth of 24% over last year, which indicates increased client billing and staff recruitment
Competition Observations: One confidential shredding company serves the region, covering Anycity and the surrounding towns Provide regular (weekly or biweekly) service, but does not have the capacity to handle large volumes at one time	**Online Research:** Anycity's biggest employment sectors are: manufacturing, tourism, food services, and professional services

TARGET MARKET:

The target market can then be described as small to medium-sized businesses in the professional sector with an annual revenue of $500K to $1M who require both regular and infrequent large volume paper shredding services.

Segmenting Your Market

Your market segments are the groups within your target market – broken down by a determinant in one of the following four categories:
- Demographics
- Psychographics
- Geographics
- Behaviors

Segmenting your target market into several more specific groups allows you to further tailor your marketing campaign and more specifically position your product or service. You may wish to divide your ad campaign into four sections and target four specific markets with messages that will most resonate with the audience.

For example, the baby clothing store may choose to segment its target market by psychographics, or lifestyle. If the larger target market is *married females with children under five, between the ages of 25 and 45, who have a household income of at least $100K annually*, it can be broken down into the following lifestyle segments:
- Fitness-oriented mothers
- Career-oriented mothers
- New mothers

With these three categories, unique marketing messages can be created that speak to the hot-buttons of each segment. The more accurate and specific you can make communications with your target market, the greater impact you will have on your revenues.

Market Segmentation Variables

Demographic	Psychographic	Geographic	Behavioristic
Age	Personality	Region	Brand Loyalty
Income	Lifestyle	Country	Product Usage
Gender	Values	City	Purchase
Generation	Attitude	Area	Frequency
Nationality	Motivation	Neighborhood	Profitability
Ethnicity	Activities	Density	Readiness to Buy
Marital Status	Interests	Climate	User Status
Family Size			
Occupation			
Religion			
Language			
Education			
Employment Type			
Housing Type			
Housing Ownership			
Political Affiliation			

Understanding Your Target Market

Once you have determined who your market is, make a point of learning everything you can about them. You need to have a strong understanding of who they are, what they like, where they shop, why they buy and how they spend their time. Remind yourself that you may *think* you know your market, but until you have verified the information, you'll be driving your marketing strategy blind.

Also be aware that markets change, just like people. Just because you knew your market when you started your business 10 years ago, doesn't mean you know it now. Regular market research is part of any successful business plan, and a great habit to start.

Types of Market Research

Surveys

The simplest way to gather information from your clients or target market is through a survey. You can craft a questionnaire full of questions about your product, service, market demographics, buyer motivations, and so on. Plus, anonymous surveys will produce the most accurate information since names are not attached to the results or specific comments.

Depending on the purpose—whether it is to gather demographic information, product or service feedback, or other data—there are a number of ways to administer a survey.

1. *Telephone*

Telephone surveys are a more time-consuming option but have the benefit of live communication with your target market. Generally, it is best to have a third-party conduct this type of survey to gather the most honest feedback. This is the method that market researchers use for polling, which is highly reliable.

2. *Online*

Online surveys are the easiest to administer yourself. There are many web-based services that quickly and easily allow to you custom create your survey, and send it to your email marketing list. These services can also analyze, summarize and interpret the results on your behalf. Keep in mind that the results include only those who are motivated to respond, which may slant your results.

3. *Paper-based.*

Paper surveys are seldom used and can prove to be an inefficient method. Like online surveys, your results are based on the feedback of those who were motivated for one reason or another to respond. However, the time and effort involved in taking the survey, filling it out, and returning it to your place of business may deter people from participating.

Keep in mind that surveys can be complex to administer, and consume more time and resources than you have planned. If you have the budget, consider hiring a professional market research firm to lead or assist with the process. This will also ensure that the methodology is standard practice, and will garner the most accurate results.

Website Analysis

Tracking your website traffic is an excellent way to research your existing and potential customer's interests and behavior. From this information, you can ensure the design, structure, and content of your website is catering to the people who use it – and the people you want to use it.

User-friendly website traffic analytics programs can easily show you who is visiting your site, where they are from, and what pages of your site they are viewing. Services like Google Analytics can tell you what page they arrive at, where they click to, how much time they spend on each page, and on which page they leave the site.

This is powerful (and free!) information to have in your market research, and easy to monitor monthly or weekly, depending on the needs of your business.

Customer Purchase Data (Consumer Behavior)

If you do not have the budget to conduct your own professional market research, you can use existing resources on consumer behavior. While this data may not be specific to your region or city, general consumer research is actual data that can be helpful in confirming assumptions you may have made about your target market.

Your customer loyalty program or Point of Sale system may also be of help in tracking customer purchases and identifying trends in purchase behavior. If you can track who is buying, what they're buying and how often they're buying, you'll have an arsenal of powerful insight into your existing client base.

Focus Groups

Focus groups look at the psychographic and behavioristic aspects of your target market. Groups of six to 12 people are gathered and asked general and specific questions about their purchase motivations and behaviors. These questions could relate to your business in particular, or to the general industry.

Focus group sessions can also be time-consuming to organize and facilitate, so consider hiring the services of a professional market research firm. You may also receive more honest information if a third-party is asking the questions, and receiving the responses from focus group participants.

For cost savings, consider partnering with an associate in the same industry who is not a direct competitor, and who would benefit from the same market data.

5

Creating a Powerful Offer

"Strive not to be a success, but rather to be of value."
- Albert Einstein

I'm not going to beat around the bush on this one:

Your offer is the granite foundation of your marketing campaign.

Get it right, and everything else will fall into place. Your headline will grab readers, your copy will sing, your ad layout will hardly matter, and you will have customers running to your door.

Get it wrong, and even the best looking, best-written campaign will sink like the Titanic.

A powerful offer is an irresistible offer. It's an offer that gets your audience frothing at the mouth and clamoring over each other all the way to your door. An offer that makes your readers pick up the phone and open their wallets.

Irresistible offers make your potential customers think, "I'd be crazy not to take him up on that," or "An offer like this doesn't come around very often." They instill a sense of emotion, of desire, and ultimately, urgency.

Make it easy for customers to purchase from you the first time, and spend your time keeping them coming back.

I'll say it again: **get it right, and everything else will fall into place.**

The Crux of Your Marketing Campaign

As you work your way through this book, you will find that nearly every chapter discusses the importance of a powerful offer as related to your marketing strategy or promotional campaign.

There's a reason for this. The powerful offer is more often than not the reason a customer will open their wallets. It is how you generate leads, and then convert them into loyal customers. The more dramatic, unbelievable, and valuable the offer is the more dramatic and unbelievable the response will be.

Many companies spend thousands of dollars on impressive marketing campaigns in glossy magazines and big city newspapers. They send massive direct mail campaigns on a regular basis, yet don't receive an impressive or massive response rate.

These companies do not yet understand that simply providing information on their company and the benefits of their product is not enough to get customers to act. There is no reason to pick up the phone or visit the store, *right now*.

Your powerful, irresistible offer can:

- Increase leads
- Drive traffic to your website or business
- Move old product
- Convert leads into customers
- Build your customer database

What Makes a Powerful Offer?

A powerful offer is one that makes the most people respond and take action. It gets people running to spend money on your product or service.

Powerful offers nearly always have an element of *urgency* and of *scarcity*. They give your audience a reason to act immediately, instead of putting it off until a later date.

Urgency relates to time. The offer is only available until a certain date, during a certain period of the day, or if you act within a few hours of seeing the ad. The customer needs to act now to take advantage of the offer.

Scarcity related to quantity. There are only a certain number of customers who will be able to take advantage of the offer. There may be a limited number of spaces, a limited number of products, or simply a limited number of people the business will provide the offer to. Again, this requires that customer acts immediately to reap the high value for low cost.

Powerful offers also:

Offer great value. Customers perceive the offer as having great value – more than a single product on its own, or the product at its regular price. It is clear that the offer takes the reader's needs and wants into consideration.

Make sense to the reader. They are simple and easy to understand if read quickly. Avoid percentages – use half off or 2 for 1 instead of 50% off. There are no "catches" or requirements; no fine print.

Seem logical. The offer doesn't come out of thin air. There is a logical reason behind it – a holiday, the end of a season, anniversary celebration, or new product. People can get suspicious of offers that seem "too good to be true" and have no apparent purpose.

Provide a premium. The offer provides something extra to the customer, like a free gift, or free product or service. They feel they are getting something extra for no extra cost. Premiums are perceived to have more value than discounts.

Remember that when your target market reads your offer, they will be asking the following questions:

1. What are you offering me?
2. What's in it for me?
3. What makes me sure I can believe you?
4. How much do I have to pay for it?

The Most Powerful Types of Offers

Decide what kind of offer will most effectively achieve your objectives. Are you trying to generate leads, convert customers, build a database, move old product off the shelves, or increase sales?

Consider what type of offer will be of most value to your ideal customers – what offer will make them act quickly.

Free Offer

This type of offer asks customers to act immediately in exchange for something free. This is a good strategy to use to build a customer database or mailing list. Offer a free consultation, free consumer report, or another item of low-cost to you but of high perceived value.

You can also advertise the value of the item you are offering for free. For example, act now and you'll receive a free consultation, worth $75 dollars. This will dramatically increase your lead generation, and allow you to focus on conversion when the customer comes through the door or picks up the phone.

The Value Added Offer

Add additional services or products that cost you very little, and combine them with other items to increase their attractiveness. This increases the perception of value in the customer's mind, which will justify increasing the price of a product or service without incurring extra hard costs to your business.

Package Offer

Package your products or services together in a logical way to increase the perceived value as a whole. Discount the value of the package by a small margin, and position it as a "start-up kit" or "special package." By packaging goods of mixed values, you will be able to close more high-value sales. For example: including a free desk-jet printer with every computer purchase.

Premium Offer

Offer a bonus product or service with the purchase of another. This strategy will serve your bottom line much better than discounting. This includes 2 for 1 offers, offers that include free gifts, and in-store credit with purchases over a specific dollar amount.

Urgency Offer

As I mentioned above, offers that include an element of urgency enjoy a better response rate, as there is a reason for your customers to act immediately. Give the offer a deadline or limit the number of spots available.

Guarantee Offer

Offer to take the risk of making a purchase away from your customers. Guarantee the performance or results of your product or service, and offer to compensate the customer with their money back if they are not satisfied. This will help overcome any fear or reservations about your product and make it more likely for your leads to become customers.

Create Your Powerful Offer

1. Pick a single product or service.

Focus on only one product or service – or one product or service *type* – at a time. This will keep your offer clear, simple, and easy to understand. This can be an area of your business you wish to grow or old product that you need to move off the shelves.

2. Decide what you want your customers to do.

What are you looking to achieve from your offer? If it is to generate more leads, then you'll need your customer to contact you. If it is to quickly sell an old product, you'll need your customer to come into the store and buy it. Do you want them to visit your website? Sign up for your newsletter? How long do they have to act? Be clear about your call to action, and state it clearly in your offer.

3. Dream up the biggest, best offer.

First, think of the biggest, best things you could offer your customers – regardless of cost and ability. Don't limit yourself to a single type of offer, combine several types of offers to increase value. Offer a premium, plus a guarantee, with a package offer. Then take a look at what you've created, and make the necessary changes so it is realistic.

4. Run the numbers.

Finally, make sure the offer will leave you with some profit – or at least allow you to break even. You don't want to publish an outrageous offer that will generate a tremendous number of leads, but leave you broke. Remember that each customer has an acquisition cost, as well as a lifetime value. The amount of their first purchase may allow you to break even, but the amounts of their subsequent purchases may make you a lovely profit.

6

Profiting from Internet Marketing

"A business without a mailing list is not a business"
- Dan Kennedy

Is your business online? If not, it should be.

The internet is today's primary consumer research tool. If your business does not have an online presence, it is harder for customers to find and choose your business over the competition. With over 73% of North Americans online, it is no wonder that individuals and businesses in all industries are looking to the internet to enhance their marketing strategies.

Luckily, it has never been easier to establish and maintain a comprehensive online presence. Internet marketing, also referred to as online marketing, online advertising or e-marketing, is the fastest growing medium for marketing.

But it is not just company websites that users are viewing. Blogs, consumer reviews, chat rooms and a variety of social media are growing rapidly in popularity.

The internet is a very powerful tool for businesses if used strategically and effectively. It can be a cost saving alternative to traditional marketing approaches and may be the most effective way to communicate with your target consumer.

A major advantage of the internet is that you are always open. Users can access your business 24 hours a day, 7 days a week, and depending on your business and the purpose of the website, visitors can also purchase goods at any time.

Internet Marketing for Everyone

The internet is a great way to create product and brand awareness, develop relationships with consumers and share and exchange information. You can't afford not be taking advantage of online marketing opportunities because your competition is likely already there.

Internet marketing can take on many different forms. By creating and maintaining a website for your business, you are reaching out to a new consumer base. You can have full control over the messaging that users are receiving, and take advantage of its global reach.

Internet marketing can be very cost-effective. If you have a strong email database of your customers, an e-newsletter may be cheaper and more effective than post mail. You can deliver time sensitive materials immediately and can update your subscribers instantaneously.

Top 10 Websites (Globally)

1.	Yahoo.com		6.	MSN.com
2.	Google.com		7.	MySpace
3.	YouTube		8.	Wikipedia
4.	Windows Live		9.	Blogger.com
5.	Facebook		10.	Yahoo Japan

You will notice that half of these websites are search engines. An increasing number of consumers are first researching products, services and companies online, whether it be to compare products, complete a sale, or look for a future employer. Most people in the 18-35 age group obtain all of their information online—including news, weather, product research, etc. The remaining sites are interactive sites where users can upload information for social networking, or information sharing.

Internet Marketing Strategies

Internet marketing – like all other elements of your marketing campaign – needs to have clear goals and objectives. Creating brand and product awareness will not happen overnight so it is important to budget accordingly, ensuring there is money set aside for maintenance of the website and analytics.

Be flexible with ideas and options—do your research first, try out different options, then test and measure the results. Metrics and evaluations can be updated almost immediately and should be monitored regularly. By keeping an eye out for what online marketing strategies are working and which are not, it will be easier to create a balanced portfolio of marketing techniques. You might find that in certain geographical areas, certain marketing strategies are more effective than others.

This list is by no means the full extent of options available for marketing online, but it is a good place to start when deciding which options are best suited to your company.

Create a website

The primary use of the internet is information seeking, so you should provide consumers with information about your company first hand. You have more control over your branding and messaging and can also collect visitor information to determine what types of internet users are accessing your website.

Search Engine Optimization

Since search engines comprise 50% of the most visited sites globally, you can go through your website to make it more search engine friendly with the aim to increase your organic search listing. An organic search listing refers to listings in search engine results that appear in order or relevance to the entered search terms.

You may wish to repeat keywords multiple times throughout your website and write the copy on your site not only with the end reader in mind but also search engines.

Remember when you design your website that any text that appears in Flash format is not recognized by search engines. If your entire website is built on a Flash platform, then you will have a poor organic search listing.

Price Per Click Advertising

If you find that visitors access your website after searching for it first on a search engine, then it may be beneficial to advertise on these websites and bid on keywords associated with your company.

These advertisements will appear at the top of the page or along the left side of the search results on a search engine. You can have control over the specific geographic area you wish to target, set a monthly budget and have the option on only being charged when a user clicks on your link.

Online Directories

Listing your business in an online directory can be an inexpensive and effective online marketing strategy.

However, you need to be able to distinguish your company from the plethora of competitors that may exist. Likely, you will need to complement this strategy with other brand awareness campaigns.

Online Ads (i.e. banner ads on other websites)

These advertisements can have positive or negative effects based on the reputation and consumer perception of the website on which you are advertising. These ads should be treated similarly to print ads you may place in local newspapers or other publications.

Online Videos

With the growing popularity of sites such as YouTube, it is evident that people love researching online and being able to find video clips of the information they are seeking. Depending on your small business, you may want to upload informational videos or tutorials about your products or services.

Blogging

Blogging can be a fun and interactive way to communicate with users. A blog is traditionally a website maintained by an individual user that has regular entries, similar to a diary. These entries can be commentary, descriptions of events, pictures, videos, and more. Companies can use blogging as a way to keep users updated on current information and allow them to post comments on your blog. If blogging is something you wish to invest in, make sure that it is regularly updated and monitored.

Top 10 Mistakes to Avoid

Failure to measure ROI

Which metrics are you using? Are your visitors actually motivated to purchase or sign up? If the benefits of your online campaign are not greater than the costs incurred, then you may wish to re-evaluate your strategy.

Poor Web Design

This can leave a poor impression of your company on the visitor. A poor design could result in frustration on the visitors' part if they are not able to easily find what they went on your site to search for and it also does not build trust. If consumers do not trust your company or your website, you will not be able to complete the sale and develop a longer relationship with that customer. You also need to include privacy protection and security when building trust.

This also includes ensuring all information on the website is current and having customer service available if users are experiencing difficulty or cannot find the information they are seeking. This could be as simple as providing a 'Contact Us' email or phone number for support.

Becoming locked into an advertising strategy early

Remember your marketing mix when creating a marketing strategy and avoid putting all of your eggs in one basket. Online marketing is a very valuable tool, but depending on your business and your target markets, other marketing campaigns may be the best option for you. Especially if this is your first time making a significant investment into your online sector. You want to be sure to remain flexible and able to adapt your strategy based on feedback received by researching and analyzing different options.

Acting without researching

Similar to becoming locked into an advertising strategy early, this mistake implies to not dutifully testing and researching different online marketing options. For example, if your target consumer is aged 65+ and you are spending all of your marketing efforts into creating a blogging website (where the average ages of bloggers are 18-35), then you are likely not going to have a successful campaign.

Assuming more visitors means more sales

You have to go back to your original goals and the purpose of your company. More visitors may not mean more sales if your website is used primarily for information, but then consumers purchase their products elsewhere. This is also vice versa. You could have an increase in sales without an increase in unique visitors if your current consumer base is very loyal and willing to spend lots of money.

Often people will collect information online about products they wish to purchase because it is easier to compare options, but they purchase in person. Even though shopping online is becoming quite popular, people still prefer to see and feel the physical product before purchasing.

Failing to follow-up with customers that purchase

Return sales can account for up to 60% of total revenue. It's no wonder that organizations are always trying to maintain loyal customers and may have customer relationship management systems in place. It is easier to get a happy customer to purchase again than it is to get a new customer to purchase once.

Not incorporating online marketing into the business plan

By ensuring that your online marketing plan is fully integrated and accurately represents your organization's overall goals and objectives, the business plan will be more comprehensive and more encompassing.

Trying to discover your own best practices

It is very beneficial to use trial and error from your company to determine the best online strategy, but do not be afraid to do your research and learn from what other companies have already figured out. There will be many cases where someone was in a very similar position as you and they may have some suggestions and secrets that they wish to share. Researching in advance can save you a great deal of time and money.

Spending too much too fast

Although it may be cheaper than traditional marketing approaches, internet marketing does have its costs. You have to consider the software and hardware designs, maintenance, distribution, supply chain management, and the time that will be required. You don't want to spend your entire marketing budget all at once.

Getting distracted by metrics that are not relevant

As we discuss in the next section, there are endless reports and measurable statistics that you can use to analyze and determine the effectiveness of your campaign. You will need to establish which statistics are actually relevant to your marketing.

Testing and Measuring Online

As with any element of your marketing campaign, you will need to track your results and measure them against your investment. Otherwise, how will you know if your online marketing is successful?

These results - or metrics – need to be recorded and analyzed as to how they impact your overall return on investment.

Some examples of metrics are:

- New account setups
- Conversion rates
- Page stickiness
- Contact us form completions

Due to the popularity of online marketing and the importance of having a strong web presence, companies have demanded more sophisticated tracking tools and metrics for their online activities. It can be very difficult to not only know what to measure but also HOW to measure.

Thankfully, it is easier than ever to get the information you need with the many types of software and services available, including Google Analytics, which are free and relatively accurate.

8 Metrics to Track

The following are the key metrics to watch for when testing and measuring your internet marketing efforts:

Conversions

How many leads has your online presence generated, and of those leads, how many were turned into sales? Ultimately, your campaign needs to have a positive impact on your business.

Regardless of the specific purpose of the campaign – from lead generation and service sign-up, to blog entries – you need to know how many customers are taking the desired action in response to your efforts. Your tracking tool will be able to provide you with this information

Spend

If you are not making a profit – or at least breaking even – from your internet marketing efforts, then you need to change your strategy. Redistribute your financial resources and reconsider your motives and objectives for your online campaign.

An easy way to do this analysis is to divide your total spend by conversions. This could also be broken down by product. You could also use a tracking tool and view reports on the 'per visit value of every click,' from every type of source. Your sources can include organic/search engine referrals, direct visit (i.e. person typed your web address into their address bar), or email/newsletter.

Attention

You need to keep a close eye on how much attention you are getting on your website. One of the best ways to analyze this would be to compare unique visitors to page views per visit to time on site. How many people are visiting, how many pages they are viewing, what pages they are viewing, and how much time they are spending on the site.

A unique visitor is any one person who visits the website in a given amount of time. For example, if Evelyn visits her online banking website daily for an entire month, over that one month period, she is considered to be one unique visitor (not 30 visitors).

You may also want to incorporate referring source as well – the places online that refer customers to your website. You'll be able to determine what referring sources offer the 'best' visitors.

Top Referrals

Know who is doing the best job of referring clients to your website – and note how they are doing this. Is it the prominence of the link? Its positioning? Or the reputation of the referring company?

Understanding where the majority of your visitors are coming from will allow you focus on those types of sources when you increase your referral sites. They also allow you to gain a better understanding of your online market – and target audience.

Bounce Rate

The bounce rate is the number of people who visit the homepage of your website but do not visit other pages. If you have a high bounce rate, you either have all the necessary information on your homepage, or you are not giving your customers a reason to click further.

In Google Analytics, view the 'content' or 'pages' report and view the column stating bounce rate.

Errors

It is very important to track the errors that visitors receive while trying to access or view your website. For example, if someone links to your website, but makes a spelling error in typing the link, your users will see an error page in their browser, and will not ultimately make it to your website.

You can also receive reports on errors that customer's make when trying to type in your website address in their browser. You may wish to buy the domains with common spelling mistakes, and link those addresses to your true homepage. This will increase overall traffic and potential conversions.

Onsite Search Terms

If you have a 'search website' function on your website, it is useful to monitor which terms users are most frequently searching. This can provide valuable insight into the user friendliness of your site and your website's navigation system. This information will be included in the traffic reporting tool.

Bailout Rates

If you provide users with the option to purchase something on your website (i.e. shopping cart), then you can track where along the purchasing process people decided not to go through with the sale.

This could be the first step of receiving the order summary and total, or further when stating shipping options. By obtaining this information, a company can reorganize or revamp their website to make the sales process more fluid and possibly encourage more purchases.

Here are the three main questions you should be asking yourself when evaluating your website presence:

- Who visits my website?
- Where do visitors come from?
- Which pages are viewed?

7

Systemizing Your Business and Developing Effective Processes

"A true business opportunity is the one that an entrepreneur invents to grow him or herself. Not to work in, but to work on."
- Michael E. Gerber

One of the biggest mistakes a business owner can make is to create a company that is dependent on the owner's involvement for the success of its daily operations. This is called working "in" your business. You're writing basic sales letters, licking stamps, and guiding staff step-by-step through each task.

There are a number of problems with this approach. One is redundancy. You're paying your staff to carry out tasks that you eventually complete. The second is poor time management. You're spending your day – at your high hourly rate – on tasks as they arise, leaving little room for the tasks you need to be focused on.

However, the biggest issue I have with this approach is that countless intelligent business owners are spending the majority of their time operating their business, instead of *growing* it.

A good test of this is to ask yourself, what would happen if you took off to a hot sunny destination for three weeks and left your cell phone, PDA and laptop at home. Would your business be able to continue operating?

If you said no, then this chapter is for you.

Systemizing your business is about putting policies and procedures in place to make your business operations run smoother – and more importantly – without your constant involvement. With your newfound free time, **you will be able to focus your efforts on the bigger picture: strategically growing your business.**

Why Systemize?

For most small business owners, systems simply mean freedom from the day-to-day functioning of their organization. The company runs smoothly, makes a profit, and provides a high level of service – regardless of the owner's involvement.

Systemizing your business is also a healthy way to plan for the future. You're not going to be working forever – what happens when you retire? How will you transition your business to new ownership or management? How will you take that vacation you've been dreaming of?

Businesses that function without their ownership are also highly valuable to investors. Systemizing your business can position it in a favorable light for purchase, and merit a high price tag.

A system is any process, policy, or procedure that consistently achieves the same result, regardless of who is completing the task.

Any task that is performed in your business more than once can be systemized. Ideally, the tasks that are completed on a cyclical basis – daily, weekly, monthly, and quarterly – should be systemized so much so that anyone can perform them.

Systems can take many forms – from manuals and instruction sheets to signs, banners, and audio or video recordings. They don't have to be elaborate or extensive, just provide enough information in the step-by-step form to guide the person performing the task.

Benefits of Business Systems

There are unlimited benefits available to you and your business through systemization. The more systems you can successfully implement, the more benefits you'll see.

- Better cost management
- Improved time management
- Clearer expectations of staff
- More effective staff training and orientation
- Increased productivity (and potentially profits)

- Happier customers (consistent service)
- Maximized conversion rates
- Increased staff respect for your time
- Increased level of individual initiative
- Greater focus on long-term business growth

Taking Stock of Your Existing Systems

The first step in systemizing your business is taking a long look at the existing systems (if any) in your business. At this point, you can look for any systems that have simply emerged as "the way we do things here."

How do your staff answer the phone? What is the process customers go through when dealing with your business? How are employees hired? Trained? How is performance reviewed and rewarded?

Some of your systems may be highly effective, and not require any changes. Others may be ineffective and require some reworking. If you have previously established some systems, now is a good time to check-in and evaluate how well they are functioning.

Use the following chart to record what systems currently exist in your business.

Existing Systems	
Administration	
Financials	
Communication	
Customer Relations	
Employees	
Marketing	
Data	

Seven Areas to Systemize

Without a doubt, system creation – especially when none exist to begin with – is a daunting and time-consuming task. For many businesses, it can be difficult to determine where to start to make the best use of their time from the onset.

Here are seven main areas of your business you can to systemize. Begin with one area, and move to the other areas as you are ready. Alternately, start with one or two systems within each area, and evaluate how those new systems affect your business. Each business will require its own unique set of systems.

1. Administration

This is an important area of your business to systemize because administrative roles tend to see a high turnover. A series of systems will reduce training time, and keep you from explaining how the phones are to be answered each time a new receptionist joins your team.

Administrative Systems	
Opening and closing procedures	Filing and paper management
Phone greeting	Workflow
Mail processing	Document production
Sending couriers	Inventory management
Office maintenance (watering plants, emptying recycle bins, etc.)	Order processing
	Making orders

2. Financials

This is one area of systems that you will need to keep a close eye on – but that doesn't mean you have to do the work yourself. Financial management systems are everything from tracking credit card purchases to invoicing clients and following up on overdue accounts.

These systems will help to prevent employee theft, and allow you to always have a clear picture of your numbers. It will allow you to control purchasing, and ensure that each decision is signed-off on.

Financial Systems	
Purchasing	Profit/loss statements
Credit card purchase tracking	Invoicing
Accounts payable	Daily cash out
Accounts receivable	Petty cash
Bank deposits	Employee expenses
Cutting checks	Payroll
Tax payments	Commission payments

3. Communications

The area of communication is essential and time-consuming for any business. Fax cover letters, sales letters, internal memos, reports, and newsletters are items that need to be created regularly by different people in your organization.

Most of the time, these communications aren't much different from one to the next, yet each is created from scratch by a different person. There is a huge opportunity for systemization in this area of your business. Systemized communication ensures consistency and company differentiation.

Communication Systems	
Internal memo template	Newsletter template
Fax cover template	Sales letter template(s)
Letterhead template	Meeting minutes template
Team meeting agenda	Report template
Sending faxes	Internal meetings
Internal emails	Scheduling

4. Customer Relations

Another important area for systemization is customer relations. This includes everything the customer sees or touches in your company, as well as any interaction they might have with you or your staff members.

Establishing a customer relations system will also ensure that new staff members understand how customers are handled in *your* business. It will allow you to maintain a high level of customer service, without constantly reminding staff of your policies. It will also ensure that the success of your customer relations and retention does not hinge on you or any other individual salesperson.

Customer Relations Systems	
Incoming phone call script	Sales process
Outgoing phone call script	Sales script
Customer service standards	Newsletter templates

Customer retention strategy Customer communications templates	Ongoing customer communication strategy Customer liaison policy

5. Employees

Create systems in your business for hiring, training, and developing your employees. This will establish clear expectations for the employee, and streamline time-consuming activities like recruitment.

Employees with clear expectations who work within clear structures are happier and more productive. They are motivated to achieve 'A' when they know they will receive 'B' if they do. Establishing a clear training manual will also save you and your staff the time and hassle of training each new staff member on the fly.

Employee Systems	
Employee recruitment	Staff uniforms or dress code
Employee retention	Employee training
Incentive and rewards program	Ongoing training and professional development
Regular employee reviews	
Employee feedback structure	Job descriptions and role profiles

6. Marketing

This is likely an area in which you spend a large part of your time. You focus on generating new leads and getting more people to call you or walk through your doors. These efforts can be systemized and delegated to other staff members.

Use the information in this program to create simple systems for your basic promotional efforts. Any one of your staff should be able to pick up a marketing manual and implement a successful direct mail campaign or place a purposeful advertisement.

Marketing Systems	
Referral program	Regular advertisements
Customer retention program	Advertisement creation system
Regular promotions	Direct mail system
Marketing calendar	Sales procedures
Enquiries management	Lead management

7. Data

While we like to think we operate a paperless office, often the opposite is true. Your business needs to have clear systems for managing paper and electronic information to ensure that information is protected, easily accessed, and only kept when necessary.

Data management systems help you keep your office organized. Everyone knows where information is to be stored, and how it is to be handled, which prevents big stacks of paper with no place to go.

Ensure that within your data management systems you include a data backup system. That way, if anything happens to your server or computer software, your data – and potentially your business – is protected.

Data Management Systems	
IT Management	Client file system
Data backup	Project file system
Computer repairs	Point of sale system
Electronic information storage	Financial data management

Implementing New Systems

If you completed the exercise earlier in this chapter, you will have a good idea of the systems that are currently in place in your business. The next step is to determine what systems you need to create in your business.

To do this you will need to get a better understanding of the tasks that you and your employees complete on a daily and weekly basis. If you operate a timesheet program, this can be a good source of information. Alternately, ask staff to keep a daily log for a week of all the tasks they contribute to or complete. Doing so will not only give you valuable insight into how they spend their time on a daily basis but also involve them in the systemizing process.

Review all task logs or timesheet records at the end of the week, remove duplicates, and group like tasks together. From here you can categorize the tasks into business areas like the seven listed above, or create your own categories.

Then, you will need to prioritize and plan your system creation and implementation efforts. Choose one from each category, or one category to focus on at a time. The amount you can take on will depend on your business needs, and the staff resources you have available to you for this process.

Remember that system creation is a long-term process – not something that will transform your business overnight. Be patient, and focus on the items that hold the highest priority.

Creating Your Systems

There is a big variety of ways you can create systems for your business – depending on the type of system you need and the type of business you operate. Some systems will be short and simple – i.e., a laminated sign in the kitchen that outlines step-by-step how to make the coffee – while others will be more complex – i.e., your sales scripts or letter templates.

One thing all of your systems have in common is steps. There is a linear process involved from start to finish. Begin by writing out each of the steps involved in completing the task, and provide as much detail as you can.

Then, review your step-by-step guide with the employee(s) who regularly complete the task and gather their feedback. Once you have incorporated their input, decide what format the system needs to be in: manual, laminated instruction sheet, sign, office memo, etc.

Testing Your Systems

Now that you have created a system, you will need to make sure that it works. More specifically, you need to make sure that it works without your involvement.

Implement the new system for an appropriate period of time – a week or month – then ask for input from staff, suppliers and vendors, and customers. Evaluate if it is informative enough for your staff, seamless enough for your suppliers, and whether or not it meets or exceeds your customer's needs.

Take that feedback and revise the system accordingly. You will rarely get the system right the first time – so be patient.

Systems will also need to be evaluated and revised on a regular basis to ensure your business processes are kept up to date. Structure an annual or bi-annual review of systems, and stick to it.

Employee Buy-In

It will be nearly impossible for you to develop effective systems without the involvement and input of your employees. These are the people who will be using the systems, and who are completing the tasks on a regular basis without systems. They have a wealth of knowledge to assist you in this process.

Employees can also draft the systems for you to review and finalize. This will make the systemization process a much faster and more efficient one.

It is also important to note that when you introduce new systems into your company, there may be a natural resistance to the change. People – including your employees – are habitual people who can become set in the way they are used to doing things.

Delegation

The final step to systemizing your business is delegation. What is the point of creating systems unless someone other than you can use them to perform tasks?

This doesn't have to mean completely removing your involvement from the process, but it does mean giving your employees enough freedom to complete the task within the structure of the systems you have spent time and considerable thought creating.

After that, allow yourself the freedom of focusing on the tasks that you most enjoy, and those that most deserve your time – like creating big picture strategies to grow your business and increase your profits.

8

How to Create Repeat Business and Have Clients that Pay, Stay and Refer

"Make a customer, not a sale."
- Katherine Barchetti

When it comes to marketing and generating more income, most business owners are focused outward.

They've carefully established and segmented their target market and created specific offers and messages for each market segment. They spend thousands of dollars on advertising and direct mail campaigns in hot pursuit of more leads, more customers, and more foot traffic.

While this is an effective way to build a business, it is costly and time-consuming. It requires constant and consistent effort, and while this approach does generate results, those results quickly disappear when the effort stops or becomes less intense.

Successful businesses that see sustained growth have a double-edged marketing strategy. They focus their efforts *outward* – on new potential customers and marketing – as well as *inward* – on existing customers and referral business.

These successful businesses have leveraged their existing efforts to generate more revenue. Simply put, their customers buy from them over and over again.

For most businesses, this is the easiest way to increase their revenues. Simple customer loyalty strategies and outstanding customer service are often all you need to dramatically increase your sales – from the customers you already have.

The Cost of Your Customers

Do you know how much it costs your business to buy new customers?

Each new customer that walks through your door – with the exception of referrals – has cost you money to acquire. You have spent money on advertising and promotions to generate leads and turn those leads into customers.

For example, if you have placed an ad in your local newspaper for $1,000, and the ad brings in 10 customers, you have paid $100 to acquire each customer. You would need to ensure each of those customers spent at least $200 to cover your margin and break-even.

Alternately, if you spent two hours of your time and $10 per month on an email marketing program to send a newsletter to your existing database of customers, and you bring in 10 customers as a result – each customer has cost you $1.

Generating more repeat business means focusing on the marketing strategies that aim to keep your existing customers instead of purchase new ones – effectively reducing the cost of attracting new customers to your business.

These strategies are simple to implement and don't require much time investment. Just a solid understanding of how to make customers want to come back and spend more of their money

Keeping Your Customers

Marketing strategies that focus on keeping your current customer base are easy and enjoyable to implement. They allow you to build real relationships with the people you do business with, instead of dealing with a revolving door of people on the other end of your sales process.

Repeat customers create a community of people around your business that presumably share the same needs, desires and frustrations. The information you gain from these customers (market research) can help you strengthen your understanding of your target audience, and more accurately segment it.

Remember – 80% of your revenue comes from 20% of your customers. Always focus on these customers. They are ideal customers that you want to recruit and hold on to.

Customer Service: Make them love buying from you

Every business – even those with excellent service standards can improve the service they provide their customers. Customer service seems to be a dying concept in most businesses; more focus seems to be placed on the speed of the transaction. These days you can even go to the grocery store now and not speak to a single sales associate thanks to self-serve checkouts.

To improve your company's customer service standards, take a survey of your customers and your employees to brainstorm ways you can improve the experience of buying from your business.

Successful customer service standards – those that make your customers *buy* – are:

Consistent. The standards are up kept by every person in your organization. Expectations are clear and followed through. Customers know what to expect, and choose your business because of those expectations.

Convenient. It is nearly effortless for the customer to spend money at your place of business. Convenience can take many forms – location, product selection, value-added services like delivery – and it is also consistent.

Customer-driven. The service the customer receives is exactly how they would like to be treated when buying your product or service. It is reflective of your target market, and appropriate to their lifestyle. Customers would probably not appreciate white linen tablecloths at a fast food restaurant, but they would appreciate a 2-minutes or less guarantee.

Newsletters: Keep in touch with your customers

A regular newsletter is an easy, time-effective, and inexpensive marketing strategy to implement. Unfortunately, many small businesses think these are too time-consuming and too expensive to adopt as part of their marketing strategy.

The most popular type of newsletter distribution is email. This will cost your business as little at $10 per month for an email marketing service subscription and can be customized to your unique branding.

Here is an easy five-step process to starting a company newsletter:

1. Pick your audience. New customers? Market segment? Existing customers?
2. Choose what you're going to say. Company news? Feature product? New offer?
3. Determine how you're going to say it. Articles? Bullet points? Pictures?
4. Decide how it's going to get to your audience. Email? Mail? In-store?
5. Track your results. How many people opened it? Read it? Took action?

Value Added Service: Give them happy surprises

Adding value to your business is an effective way of getting your customers back. Every person I know would choose a mattress store that offered free delivery over one that did not. It's that simple.

There are many ways to add value to your business, including:

o **Feature your expertise.** Use your knowledge to provide additional value to your customers. Offer a free consumer guide or report with every purchase.

o **Add convenience services.** Offer a service that makes their purchase easier, or more convenient. The best example of this is free shipping or delivery.

o **Package complementary services**. Packaging like items together creates an increase in perceived value. This is great for start-up kits.

o **Offer new products or services**. Feature top of the line or exclusive products, available only at your business. Offer a new service or profile a new staff member with niche expertise.

Value added services generate repeat customers in one of two ways:

1. Impress them on their first visit. Impress your customer with great service, a product that meets their needs, and then wow them with something extra that they weren't expecting. Get them to associate the experience of dealing with your business with happy surprises, and create a perception of higher value.

2. Entice them to come back. The introduction of a new value-added service can be enough to convince a customer to buy from you again. Their initial purchase established a trust and knowledge of your business and its processes. They will want to "be included" in anything new you have to offer – especially if there is exclusivity. It is easier to attract clients that have purchased from you than potential clients who have not.

Customer Loyalty Programs: Give them incentives

Another simple way to keep in touch with existing customers and keep them coming back to you is to create a customer loyalty program.

These programs do not have to be complicated or costly and are relatively easy to maintain once they have been implemented. These programs help you gain more information on your customers and their purchasing habits.

Here are some examples of simple loyalty programs that you can implement:

Free product or service. Give them every 10th (or 6th) product or service free. Produce stamp cards with your logo and contact information on it.

Reward dollars. Give them a certain percentage of their purchase back in money that can only be spent in-store. Produce "funny money" with your logo and brand.

Rewards points. Give them a certain number of points for every dollar they spend. These points can be spent in-store, or on special items you bring in for points only.

Membership amenities. Give members access to VIP amenities that are not available to other customers. Produce member cards or give out member numbers.

Remember that in order for this strategy to work, you and your team have to understand and promote it. The program in itself becomes a product that you sell.

9

Risk Reversal to Increase Sales

"It's much easier to double your business by doubling your conversion rate than by doubling your traffic."
- Jeff Eisenberg

What is the biggest objection you need to overcome when closing a sale? Is it cost? Belief in what you have to say? Confidence in your product or service?

While it is a different answer for every business, every business has to deal with some element of customer fear or hesitation before a monetary transaction.

The reality is that even if you overcome these objections and close the sale, your customer walks away carrying 99% of the risk associated with the purchase. If the product doesn't work, breaks down, or doesn't perform to expectations, your customer has parted with their dollars in exchange for disappointment.

In marketing, your objective is to generate as many leads as possible, then to convert each lead into a customer, or sale. The ratio of leads to closed sales is called your conversion rate.

What if you could eliminate the risk involved in a transaction? Would you turn more leads into customers? The answer is, "absolutely".

Introducing a risk reversal element into your marketing message or unique offer is a powerful way to give yourself an edge on the competition and close more sales. But how exactly are you going to do this?

It's easy – just give them a guarantee.

The Power of Guarantees

What is Risk Reversal?

Risk reversal simply refers to reversing the risk associated with a transaction – transferring it from the customer to the vendor.

Everyone can think of a handful of times they have purchased a product or service that did not deliver on their expectations. A time where a salesperson made them a promise and did not deliver. A time where they *lost money* on a faulty product or bogus service.

Fear of being burned or taken advantage of prevents many people from spending their money. Customers can also be very wary of buying a product or service for the first time.

Providing a strong guarantee eliminates the majority of risk involved in the purchase, and breaks down natural barriers in the sales process. Guarantees will often shorten the sales process altogether – skipping any discussion of objections – because the customer does not see any risk in "trying the product out."

There is also a growing consumer expectation when it comes to guarantees. Many stores will take back anything the customer has not been happy with, and return money or store credit. Popular health food stores encourage customers to try new or unfamiliar products by promising a hassle-free, no questions asked return process. A guarantee or easy return policy can be the difference between choosing one business over its competition.

Your customers buy results, not products or services

The strongest guarantee you can make is on *results*, not products or services.

If you guarantee that your customer will receive the benefits or results they are looking for, the specific product or service they'll need to achieve those results becomes irrelevant.

People buy benefits and results. For example, they don't buy water purifiers; they buy the benefit of enjoying clean, fresh-tasting water. They don't buy lawn sprinkler systems; they buy a healthy green lawn.

Once you understand what specific benefit or solution your customers are seeking, find a way to guarantee they'll receive or experience that solution. If they don't, you'll compensate them for it.

Remember what you have guaranteed

While guarantees will increase sales for most businesses, they can also be the fast track to business failure if their product or service isn't a quality one. Take the time to ensure you have a strong offering before you implement a guarantee.

Guarantees are most effective when you are selling someone something they need or want – not when you are trying to convince someone to purchase something they have no use for.

Increasing Conversion Rates with a Guarantee

Guarantees can help your business turn more qualified leads into repeat customers. Strong guarantees are big and bold, but also realistic. They're just a little bit better than your competition but consistent with the industry's standards.

Your conversion rate

Your conversion rate is the percentage of clients you convert from leads into customers. The higher your conversion rate, the more revenue you will generate.

To figure out your conversion rate, divide the number of people who purchase from you by the number of people who inquired about your product or service. This will generate a percentage value of your conversion rate.

Guarantees encourage and increase conversion. They motivate potential customers to buy – and to buy from you – because you stand behind what you sell in a big way. There is no risk involved in purchasing what you have to offer.

Creating your guarantee

So you're convinced your business – and your customers – would benefit from a strong guarantee. Now what? What are you going to guarantee? How are you going to position it?

Once again, this goes back to your target audience and your product or service. What are some of the major objections your potential customers raise during the sales process? What kind of risk do they take on when they make a purchase? How much time will they need to test or experience your product or service?

Brainstorm a list of things about your industry that really frustrate your customers. They could be service-based (contractors that don't show up, employees who don't perform) or product-based (products that break, do not perform). Then, take a look at your list and decide how you can make sure these things do not happen. Think big – you can do a lot more than you think – then determine if you can actually make good on your promise. If you can't guarantee the first frustration, then move on to the second.

Here are some tips on writing your guarantee:

- **Be specific**. Explain exactly what you are guaranteeing. Don't make vague guarantees that a product will "work" or a service will make you "happy". These words mean different things to different people. Guarantee specific performance or results.

- **Include a clear timeframe.** Put a realistic timeframe on your guarantee. Very few products or services are good forever. Offer a 30-day or 90-day free trial; guarantee results within a set number of days or weeks. This can protect your company and sets out clear expectations for your clients.

- **Be bold**. Unbelievable guarantees get a customer's attention, so go as far as you realistically can with your claim. Find a way to stand out from the competition – which may also have a guarantee.

- **Tell them what you'll do**. Explain what you'll do – how you'll compensate them – if your product or service doesn't deliver. Be specific, talk money, and go above and beyond.

Implementing guarantees

Tell your clients!

Put your guarantee everywhere – your website, brochures, receipt tape, in-store signage, advertisements, and other promotional materials. It will only help attract customers if they know about it.

Send a newsletter to your existing client base informing them of your new guarantees – you never know how many customers you can convince to come back and spend more in your business.

Train your Staff

Once you have decided to offer your clients a guarantee, you need to ensure your staff is properly trained on the specific policies and procedures associated with that guarantee. If you offer different guarantees for different products and services, ensure this is made clear as well.

Presumably, your staff will be communicating the details of your guarantee and fielding customer questions. They will have to know how to sell the product using the guarantee as a benefit and understand every application of the guarantee in your business. Every scenario a customer may need to use it.

To ensure your staff is not making any false claims or promises, create a guarantee script for them to use and stick to. This will prevent customers from returning with false hopes for their money back, or other compensation.

Returns + Claims

So, by now you must be thinking, "Great, I can convert more customers with a strong guarantee, and increase my sales. But what about the added risk I have taken on from my customers? Won't I start to see a ton of returns and service claims?" This is a valid question. Making a strong guarantee means standing by it and delivering on your promise. Inevitably, when you guarantee something, someone is going to take you up on that guarantee and make a claim. I'm going to answer this question in two parts:

1. Stand behind your product or service. You're not in business to scam customers. If you sell a product or service, and you believe in it enough to offer it to your customers, it is likely a quality product or genuine service.

If this is a concern to you, consider implementing strong quality controls or stronger criteria for your merchandising. Companies that offer products and services that deliver results can offer the strongest guarantees.

Of course, you will get returns. You will have customers come in to take advantage of you. Just remember that as long as the increase in sales outweighs the claims, your guarantee strategy has been successful.

2. Understand your customer's likely behavior. The truth is that most customers will never take advantage of your guarantee – regardless of their satisfaction level. There are a number of reasons for this.

The first is that most people can't be bothered to drive, mail, or otherwise, seek a refund on an item under $50. Many let the timeframe slip by and have an "oh well" attitude.

The second is that most people don't like confrontation. There is usually an element of confrontation involved in telling someone you didn't like a product or service, and many people do not have the confidence to do so. They'd rather eat the cost than going through the process of asking for a refund.

Handling claims and returns:

If you do have your product returned, it is in your company's best interest to create a system for handling these customer interactions.

Create a claim form

Ensure that each customer who makes a claim about your product or service fills out a standard form. Doing so will help you prevent fraud, gather important information about the customer and their reasoning, and create a "hoop" for the customer to jump through if they want their money back.

Name
Date
Contact Information
Salesperson
Product
Reason for claim:
Comments
Follow-up

Keep a claim or return log

Create a log or filing system for your claims. This will give you a snapshot of your guarantee program, a record-keeping system, and a wealth of information about each customer's experience and motivations.

Use the information

Take the claim forms your customers have filled out, and review them regularly. While some of the claims won't be genuine, there will be some real feedback you can use to improve your product or service or to modify your guarantee. You may need to make it more realistic or change the specifics.

10

Profits from Fresh Air

"Today's tactical victory does not guarantee tomorrow's strategic success."
- Peter Pace

As a small business owner, you are in business for one reason: to make money.

Of course, there are other reasons you started or purchased your company. You may love the product you sell or service you provide. You may love the challenge of turning a floundering company into an overnight success. You may just love being your own boss.

Naturally, this all means nothing if you are not generating enough income to support yourself and your family, as well as the people who work for you.

Nearly all businesses make money. Unless not a single product or service is sold, there is always money coming in. But there is also always money going out. Supplies, wages, marketing, acquisitions and operations all contribute to the expense of just staying in business.

Simply put, profit is the difference between money in and money out. This is the dollar value of your sales, minus the cost of those sales.

In business, you will find that everyone wants to make more money. They want to increase their sales, get more money coming in. **What often gets overlooked is that the true secret to making more money is not increasing sales, but increasing profit.**

What is Profit?

Before you can take steps to increase the profitability of your business, you need a solid understanding of:

- types of profit
- what factors influence profit
- what your profit is *right now*

Types of Profit

There are two main types of profit:

Gross Profit

Gross profit is the simplest form of calculating profit. It is simply the money that comes through the cash register, minus the cost of acquiring or providing the products or services.
The formula is:

Total revenue (sales) – cost of goods or services sold = Gross Profit

Net Profit

Net profit is a more accurate reflection of your income. It is calculated by taking your gross profit minus expenses over a specific time period (usually by quarter).

The formula is:

Gross profit – expenses (cost of running a business) = Net Profit

Factors that Influence Profit

Profit is your bottom line. It is the number that falls out the bottom when all other costs and expenses have been taken into consideration. Do you know what contributes to the amount of profit your business ends up with?

There are three main factors that influence profit:

Sales – Your Conversion Rate

The first and most obvious factor is the money that comes in the door through sales. In theory, the more sales you make and the more money you bring in, the greater your profits.

The ratio of potential customers to sales is called your conversion rate. This is the percentage of customers you have converted from leads to sales. So, a high conversion rate means more sales, and more money coming in the door.

In addition to your conversion rate is the lifetime value of your clients. It costs much less to convince a customer to make repeat purchases than it does to acquire new clients.

Costs – Your Product/Service Margins

The second factor is the cost of your offering – what your product or service costs you to acquire or provide. If you sell a product, this is the wholesale price you pay for the product. If you offer a service, it is the cost of your (or your employee's) time plus any materials used.

Your margin is the difference between the price you pay and the price your customers pay. If you buy toothpaste for $1 from the wholesaler, and you sell it for $3, your margin is $2. If a haircut costs $20 in materials and service, and the customer pays $50, your margin is $30.

Expenses – The Cost of Doing Business

The final factor is the cost of running your business – those not directly related to the specific product or service you offer. Expenses include:
- Office or store lease
- Computer equipment lease
- Employee salaries
- Utilities
- Marketing + advertising

Your Profit

It only makes sense that you need to know where you are to determine how to get to where you want to be. This applies to any plan you create in business.

Before you can increase your profits, you need to have an understanding of where those profits are currently – and if you're making any at all. The next section will take you through a process to review the specific factors that affect your business's profitability, and ultimately determine how much profit you are currently bringing in.

Taking Stock of Your Profits

Before you devise a strategy to increase your profits, you need to take a good long look at the money your business brings in, and the money you spend to run your business. You may wish to sit down with your accountant or bookkeeper to analyze the financial information that is available to you.

Decide on a specific time period to review – one that makes sense to your business, and one that will give you the most realistic picture of your business performance.

This will depend if your operation is cyclical, or remains steady throughout the year. Usually, the previous quarter or the previous four quarters will give you enough of an indication.

Here is a list of general items to review:

- Total revenue
- Total cost of goods or services
- Total cost of operations (overhead), including:
- Employee wages
- Recruitment
- Business development
- Utilities
- Rent or mortgage
- Office supplies
- Computer leases
- Incidentals
- Total cost of marketing campaigns

Total profit after costs and expenses for this time period: _____.

The Five Factors that Eat Your Profits

It is easy for business owners to compare their organizations to the apparent success of their competitors. Joe's Pizza may always be teaming with customers and appear to be making money hand over fist, while your pizza shop may have slower, but more steady business.

It is important to remember that a business with extraordinary sales figures is not necessarily a profitable one. Sales are just one element of your profit calculation.

Here are some other elements to think about when reviewing the profitability of your business:

Impulse Spending

How often do you make purchases for your business operations? I'm not talking about acquiring new goods and services, but upgrading computers, taking your team out for lunch or leasing a new photocopier.

Do you allow your staff to make purchases on your behalf? Who reviews these decisions? Take a look not only at *what* you buy but *how* spending is structured in your company.

Small Margins

As we discussed in the previous section, your margins are the difference between your cost and the customer's cost to purchase your goods or services.

Typically, businesses that offer a variety of products will have both products with large margins, and products with small margins. The products with large margins generate the most income, so these are the products that staff should be focused on selling.

What many businesses overlook is that products with small margins will never generate a high level of income, no matter how many you sell. A store stocked with small margin items will never be able to increase their profit because they have so little margin to work with.

Your Customers

This may seem like a backward way of thinking. Your customers spend money, so they are a positive factor in your profit calculation, right?

This is true for most of your customers. But remember the 80/20 rule of business – 80% of your revenue comes from 20% of your customers. These are your top 20% or ideal customers. What about your bottom 20%? The group of clients who ask for the moon and never stop complaining.

These clients can be a huge drain on both your staff resources and your financial resources. Their true value to your business is minimal – they cost more than they bring in. Fire them!

Loan Interest

How many business loans do you currently have? Credit card debt? Overdraft? The interest you pay on these loans can be a substantial monthly cost to your business.

A loan from a bank is just like any other product. You can shop around for the best deal. Consider consolidating or restructuring your debt to minimize interest payments. Plan to search around for the best rate on a regular basis – every few months or quarter.

Vendors

Do you purchase your goods and services from a wholesaler or retailer? How long have you been in business with this company? What do you pay for goods and services relative to your competitors?

Ensure that you are dealing with as direct a vendor as possible to minimize your acquisition costs and increase your margins. If you have been doing business with a particular vendor for an extended period of time, consider renegotiating your business arrangement.

The Basics of Increasing Profit

Your Profitability Goal

Now that you have an understanding of the current profitability of your company, it is time to look at ways to increase your bottom line.

Like all other aspects of your business development, you need to have a clear idea of your intention or purpose before you begin any activity. Assuming you wish to increase the profitability of your business, you need to determine by how much and within what time frame.

Create a profit-related goal for your business, and write it here:

_____

_____

Three Ways to Increase Profit

There are countless strategies for increasing profit, but ultimately you can only increase profit in one of three ways:

1. Get More Customers

Use marketing outreach strategies to generate more leads, and convert those leads into more customers. Introduce a new offer, expand your target audience, or approach a new target audience.

2. Get Your Customers to Buy More Often

Use customer loyalty and retention strategies to get your existing customers to buy from you more often. Make it easy for them to come back and do business with you.

You can do this by adding value to your product or service, keeping in touch on a regular basis, and giving your customers incentive to make repeat purchases. Customer service is also an overlooked component of building a repeat client base.

3. Increase How Much Your Customers Buy

You'll naturally increase your sales when you increase the number of customers and how often they purchase. The final way you can impact your profit is by increasing the average dollar value of each sale.

This can be achieved by up-selling every customer, creating package offers, and finding ways to increase the perceived value of your offering to justify increasing the price.

Managing Costs

One important way to impact the profitability of your business is through cost or spending management. Controlling how much money goes out will help you ensure that more money stays in your bank account.

Remember, however, that cutting costs can only help increase your profits so much. There is a point where you will no longer be able to reduce expenses, and you will have to focus on increasing sales.

Why Cut Costs?

Cost management may seem like an obvious way of maintaining a healthy business, but it is also one of the primary reasons 80% of small businesses fail. Overspending is a huge problem for most businesses – and they don't even realize it.

Reducing costs is a great short-term strategy to boost profits. As I mentioned above, there is a limited amount of impact cost management can have on the bottom line, so it is an ineffective long-term strategy.

Cost management can also help you to generate more capital. A business that closely monitors and controls its spending is a much more desirable candidate for a loan than a business that spends freely.

Most importantly, this strategy will help keep your business profitable through high and low periods. It's easy to spend money when your company is doing well, but this leaves little in the "just in case" account for downturns in the economy or unexpected expenses.

Where Can I Cut Costs?

Financing

As I mentioned, interest rates are a big culprit when it comes to eating profits. Take stock of how much money you are spending on a monthly basis in loan and interest payments. Can this be reduced? Is there another bank that will offer you a lower rate? Is there a way to consolidate these loans into a single, low-interest account?

Alternatively, if your business is doing well and has a large amount of money sitting in the bank; consider investing it or placing it in a high-interest savings account. Let your money make you money instead of spending it on unnecessary business luxuries.

Suppliers or Vendors

Again, as mentioned above, make sure the price you pay for goods and services – for resale of internal use – is the lowest you can find. Try to deal directly with the manufacturer or distributor, and renegotiate discounts and contracts with your vendors every year.

Hours of Operation

Evaluate the hours you are open for business each day, and why you have chosen the specific timeframe. Is it to compete with the competitors? Is it because you can serve the highest number of customers? Each hour you are open for business costs you money, so make sure you are operating under an ideal timeframe.

Staffing, Wages, and Compensation

This can be a sensitive subject for any business owner or employee. It is important to look at staffing redundancies and capacity levels – as well as hiring needs – when evaluating cost management strategies.

Do you need to hire new staff, or can you build capacity within your existing employees? Is there another way to compensate staff, or provide performance incentives that are non-monetary, have a high perceived value, and inexpensive for your business? Remember to take time and care when implementing any changes in this area of cost management.

Place of Business

If you operate an office in a downtown metropolis, you are going to have substantially higher operating costs than a competitor who runs an office just outside the city limits.

Make sure you can justify your location and the amount of money you spend to be there. Consider the following questions:

- Are my customers impacted by where I do business?
- Do my customers need to visit my office?
- What impression does my business need to present?
- Do I need parking facilities?
- Do I need to be visible?
- Do I have the staff to employ?
- Am I near public transit, lunch outlets, and other amenities?
- Do I need access after business hours?
- Should I lease or buy?
- Are there other costs specific to this location?

Eliminate the invisible!

What could you and your staff live without? What wouldn't you notice if it just disappeared one day? Take stock of expenses that are not being properly used or appreciated. Think of amenity-based items, or convenience costs, like:

- Gym Memberships
- Morning refreshments (muffins, donuts, etc.)
- Publication Subscriptions
- Designer coffee and tea
- Fancy collateral packaging

Your Pricing Strategy

The cost of your goods and services have a direct impact on the money you bring in. Your pricing strategy is so important to your business that it can even determine your success.

Deciding how much to charge for your product or service is a challenging task. You need to factor in your own costs, the product or service's perceived value and the going rate. Ultimately, you want to be able to charge as much as possible for each item, without overpricing yourself out of business.

Avoid the Lowest Pricing Strategy

The days of the lowest price guarantee and pricing wars are over, especially for small businesses. The "big players" in the marketplace will quickly put you out of business if you try to compete on price. Their pockets are deeper and they have lower operating costs due to their sheer size. They can afford to – you can't.

Clearly Position Your Company and Your Offering

How do you want your target market to view your business and your products? Are you trying to create an image of high quality? High value? Reliable service? Make sure your pricing is consistent with the image you are trying to project. If you are operating a high-end spa – you're not competing with the budget nail salon down the street, so your prices should be considerably higher.

Have a Good Working Understanding of Your Margins

Know how much the product or service costs you to offer before you establish a price. Do these costs remain consistent, or do they fluctuate? Restaurants that offer high-quality meat and seafood often price their meals at "market rates" as opposed to fixed rates. Calculate the fixed and variable costs associated with your product or service. You will want to work the cost of the product or service, a percentage of your overhead, and your own profit into the cost of each item.

Pay Attention to Factors Beyond Your Control

Be aware of any government or industry regulations on the price of your product or services. Some laws will actually limit how much you can charge for standard services. For medical and dental services, most insurance companies will put a cap on how much a customer will be compensated for each service. Seek out all external factors that could impact your pricing.

Price with a Purpose

Your pricing strategy should be purpose focused. What exactly are you trying to do by setting your prices at certain levels? Here are some potential reasons for pricing strategies:
- Short-term profit increase
- Long-term profit increase
- Customer generation
- Product positioning
- Revenue maximization
- Increase margins
- Market differentiation
- Survival

Pricing Strategies

Cost Plus Pricing

This is the most basic pricing strategy. Set your price at a number that includes:

- Cost of goods or services, based on a specific sales volume
- Percentage of expenses
- Profit margin (markup)

Target ROI Pricing

Set your price at a rate that will achieve a specific Return on Investment target. If you need to make $20,000 from 1,000 units – or $20 per unit – then set your price at $20 more than cost, plus expenses.

Value Based Pricing

This can be a bit of an arbitrary pricing strategy, but it can also be the most profitable. Set your price based on the value or added benefit it brings to a customer. For example, if your product only costs you $40 to produce, but will save the customer $2,000 per year in energy costs, a price of $150 or $200 would not appear to be unreasonable in the eyes of the customer.

Psychological Pricing

What messages are you trying to send the customer when they're looking at your prices for your products? Do you offer the best deal? The highest value? These are reasons to choose prices that are higher or lower than the competition.

Pricing Guidelines

Price higher than cost. This may seem obvious, but ensure that your pricing not only covers your costs but potential fluctuations in sales volume and in the marketplace. If you sell half of your order, will you still make a profit?

Include expenses. If you price to cover your costs, will you also be able to cover your expenses and still see a profit? Your margin needs to pay for your expenses, leave you with something to live on, plus some working capital for the company.

Consider the 'fair' price. What do your consumers think is 'fair' for each service or product? This is impacted by your competitor's price, your company's image (high quality or high value, low cost), and the perceived value of your product or service.

Strategies to Increase Profit

Once you have a concrete understanding of where your business stands today in terms of profitability, you've minimized your operating costs, and restructured your pricing strategy, you can now focus on other strategies to increase profit.

There are countless strategies and tactics that will help you to bring in more customers, get those customers to come back, and get those customers to spend more when they do.

Here is a list of ideas, many of which are covered in detail in other sections of this book:
- Advertise
- Establish an online presence
- Sell more high margin items
- Generate more leads
- Focus on referral business

- Increase customer loyalty and repeat business
- Increase conversion rates
- Restructure your team
- Reinvent your product
- Sell your intellectual capital

So What Do You Do From Here?

Take Action! If you're already an accomplished business owner and earning in excess of $250,000.00 per year (rich according to the Federal Government), use this book for direction to enhance the speed of your business success. If you are not as accomplished as you would like to be then the smartest thing to do is…

    A. Maintain Focus – But it isn't enough to focus on just a few activities, you must be sure they are the right activities

    B. Embrace Change – Keep an open mind, expand your awareness and innovate

    C. Know You Are in Good Company – Being an entrepreneur can be lonely. Find a way to run your business on your own, but not alone.

Concentrate on strategies to LEARN and the EARN will follow! If you are serious about taking the next step then go to work on yourself, study other business successes, understand marketing strategies and become a sponge for new (proven) material. The amazing thing about the game of business is that when you develop the leadership processes that allow you to effectively lead and continue to follow them, an abundance of success will follow. The biggest mistake is to start a process and then fall back into your old habits after a short time.

Above all, get the knowledge you need before you step onto the field. Think about it... if you were going to challenge Michael Jordan to a game of H O R S E Shootout for money, wouldn't it make sense to learn the game and practice before you stepped on the court to play him? It is amazing to me how many new small business people start the game of business against seasoned professionals (the competition), without first developing the necessary knowledge to be successful. Then they fail and blame the market, the economy, their location, etc.

If you have a business and have not yet managed to start to create wealth and systems that allow you to take time off, build retirement accounts or pay for your children's college, then learn and master the steps outlined in my book. I am a huge advocate of education and mentorship. Get the right information, find someone that knows how to walk you through them and watch your quality of life take new shape.